The Ten Principles Behind Great Customer Experiences

The Ten Principles Behind Great Customer Experiences

Matt Watkinson

PEARSON

Harlow, England • London • New York • Boston • San Francisco • Toronto • Sydney
Auckland • Singapore • Hong Kong • Tokyo • Seoul • Taipei • New Delhi
Cape Town • São Paulo • Mexico City • Madrid • Amsterdam • Munich • Paris • Milan

PEARSON EDUCATION LIMITED

Edinburgh Gate
Harlow CM20 2JE
Tel: +44 (0)1279 623623
Website: www.pearson.com/uk

First published 2013 (print and electronic)

© Matt Watkinson 2013 (print and electronic)

The right of Matt Watkinson to be identified as author of this work has been asserted by him in accordance with the Copyright, Designs and Patents Act 1988.

Pearson Education is not responsible for the content of third-party internet sites.

ISBN: 978-0-273-77508-9 (print)
    978-0-273-77599-7 (PDF)
    978-0-273-77598-0 (ePub)

British Library Cataloguing-in-Publication Data
A catalogue record for this book is available from the British Library

Library of Congress Cataloging-in-Publication Data
Watkinson, Matt.
    The ten principles behind great customer experiences / Matt Watkinson.—1 Edition.
        pages cm
    ISBN 978-0-273-77508-9 (pbk.)—ISBN (invalid) 978-0-273-77599-7 (PDF)—
    ISBN 978-0-273-77598-0 (ePub)
    1. Customer services.   2. Customer relations.   3. Consumer satisfaction.   I. Title.
HF5415.5.W385 2012
658.8'12--dc23

                                                                    2012039517

10 9
16

Print edition typeset in Frutiger LT Pro 10.25/14pt by 3
Printed by Ashford Colour Press Ltd, Gosport

This book is dedicated to the memory of my mother
Annette Marie Watkinson
27 October 1951 – 13 April 2010

Praise for *The Ten Principles Behind Great Customer Experiences*

ǁ Crack open the spine, and the prose reveals a cerebral and often original approach to design, customer service and management. Matt Watkinson references playwrights, directors and philosophers, and makes their theories applicable to the world of customer experiences.

SOPHIE GROVE, BUSINESS EDITOR, MONOCLE

ǁ Businesses and governments are obsessed with setting metrics. These are almost always numerical representations of some objective reality. And that's where the problem lies. First of all because such metrics can almost always be gamed. But also because they often translate badly into subjective experience. Finally here is a book which tackles this problem and has simple, practical principles for solving it. It is part of a whole movement in social science and marketing which leads me to believe – and indeed to hope – that the next revolution will be not technological but psychological.

RORY SUTHERLAND, VICE-CHAIRMAN OF OGILVY UK AND TED SPEAKER

Contents

About the author

Matt Watkinson is a designer and consultant who helps businesses get their customer experience right. He has worked with household names, design agencies and management consultancies at home in the UK, in Europe and America. Learn more about Matt at www.mattwatkinson.co.uk

Preface

At school I was always fascinated by physics. Aside from a keen interest in machines and mechanical toys that lingers on to this day, I liked the idea that there were some solid principles that even the most complex engineering challenges could be traced back to. When it comes to planes, trains and automobiles, the laws of physics make a great starting point for engineers faced with a new challenge, and can also be used to bring structure to problem solving if a solution fails.

Other passions of mine – photography and music – have their own laws too. Far from constraining creativity, they enable it by providing the artist with a structure to work within. Many seem to have an instinctive grasp of these principles from the start, but even if they don't, through diligent study and practical application they can become instinctive. They are often broken to great effect, but consciously so, with an intention in mind.

In his legendary strategy manual *The Book of Five Rings*, the samurai Miyamoto Musashi distinguishes between what he calls a 'strike' and a 'hit'. A strike, he says, is conscious and deliberate, whereas a hit is not (even if it has the desired effect of killing your opponent).[1]

Designing a mechanical object starting from the laws of physics is striking. Tinkering with things in the hope to improve performance is hitting. Striking allows repeatable success; hitting is inefficient at best, and a lottery at worst.

A few years ago I began to develop a nagging sense of unease that, more often than not, what customers experience is the product of hitting rather than striking. We are not, in most cases, basing our decisions on a theoretical understanding of how the brain works in the way that engineers use the laws of physics. The poor quality of most customer experiences is evidence enough for that.

Instead, what we end up with is a mix of a designer's subconscious feel for what is right, the subjective opinions of stakeholders, with a healthy dollop of dogma. Endless workshops, brainstorming sessions and 'alignment meetings' have become the norm in large organisations, and yet it is my experience that they are more about everyone getting to have their say, rather than a means to creating a better end result. We've ended up compensating for our lack of theoretical understanding with ever more sophisticated (and expensive) data analysis tools and elaborate, long-winded design processes.

As customers we end up suffering with experiences that are frustrating, disappointing or often infuriating. Businesses are paying the price too – quite literally – in the awesome amounts of time and other resources that it ends up costing them.

This book is about changing all that. It presents ten simple principles that can be used to improve your products and services, whatever they may be, and whatever scale you operate at. I've seen them at work everywhere from my local café to multi-billion-pound enterprises. They can be used to identify areas for improvement in current offerings, or to generate completely new ideas. They can be applied with a broad brush, or to a very small, specific issue. You are most probably using many of them without even realising it. If you are a designer or already an expert in this area, you can use them to complement your existing ways of working.

The principles are drawn from psychological theory, and while I am not a psychologist myself, my experiences as a design consultant certainly validate them, as do the examples I've included, which I hope will provide inspiration.

I also hope to demonstrate that creating a great experience for your customers doesn't have to be expensive. It doesn't require an army of boffins, and it doesn't need high-tech equipment and fancy processes. It just needs conscious, deliberate and structured thought. Most of all, it is not the sole domain of specialists. By following these principles, anyone in any business should be able to contribute to making their customers' lives that little bit easier.

Matt Watkinson
Moulsford, Oxfordshire
24 June 2012

Acknowledgements

Writing a book is much more of a team effort than many realise, and credit is due to the following. First of all to my agent John Syfret, also Patrick Walsh and Kathryn White who helped bring structure to my initial ideas; John Watkinson, Howard Watkinson, Mikael Reichel and Ben Smith, who took the time to read my early drafts – the end result is immeasurably better for their input; and the authors who took the time to respond to my queries about their work, notably Stephen Bayley, Rob Walker, Robert Hoekman Jr and Christopher Wickens. I'd also like to thank Vanessa Donnelly who has acted as a soundboard to develop my thinking over the last three years; Arthur Nurse for his excellent graphic design work; the editorial team at Pearson, especially Christopher Cudmore. The support of friends, family and colleagues has been invaluable: Martha Wiltshire, Mike 'Bomber' Reynolds, Claire Durrant, Ben Wall, Rob Syfret, Will Baker, Panos Damaskinidis, Bernard Grenville-Jones and Will Skjott. Finally, to my mum Annette Watkinson who taught me so much, not least of all that life is short – the time to start that project you always dreamed of completing is now.

Introduction

What this book is about

This book presents ten simple principles that you can use to make improvements to any customer experience. Whether you provide a product or service, are a large or small operation, a physical shop or web-based, it doesn't matter, these principles are universal.

This is a *doing* book – the emphasis is very much on practical things that you could do today, to make a real difference to the lives of your customers. To put these principles to work requires no previous expertise or experience, there is no jargon or filler, and where complex concepts arise they are presented in a manner that is accessible and simple to understand. It is my hope that small business owners, would-be entrepreneurs who dream of starting their own business, design professionals, managers and leaders will find it useful.

The advice is based on years of practical experience working with organisations from small local businesses and start-ups through to multi-national, multi-billion-pound turnover companies, in sectors as diverse as advertising, health, transport, travel, finance and telecoms. That said, I will ask you to take little on trust: the key points are all underpinned by rigorous theory from fields as wide ranging as psychology, philosophy, design and business management.

What is the 'customer experience'?

There is no one agreed definition of what is meant by the term 'customer experience' so before we go any further, here is my personal attempt at providing a useful definition:

> *The customer experience is the qualitative aspect of any interaction that an individual has with a business, its products or services, at any point in time.*

I'd like to break this definition down a bit and explain how I came to phrase it this way.

I use the term *qualitative* to reflect the fact that an experience is *perceived* by an individual's sensory and psychological faculties: it is not something that can be measured quantitatively like profit, cost, weight or task completion times. To put it another way, the experience isn't about what something does, it's *how it does it*. It's not what the features and functions of the product or service allow us to do, it's how it makes us feel.

Rather than 'customer', I prefer to use the term *individual* in my definition. Many of the most important interactions with a business take place before you actually become a customer – like looking around a shop, waiting to be served or seeing an advert. This is why many web or software designers use the term *user experience* to reflect that the person interacting with the product or service may not actually be a customer as such. I use *individual* instead of *user* since the scope of the book extends beyond websites and software to include any product or service.

It is important to clarify that the customer experience is not restricted to the usage of a product or service: it spans *every interaction* that a customer has with a business or its offerings. This can be anything from seeing an advert through to cancelling a contract, or disposing of a product when it is no longer of use. As we will see, there are many interactions that are commonly neglected but offer great opportunities to stand out from the competition. Furthermore, since the experience involves every interaction, it cannot be restricted to any period in time, or any defined point in the relationship that the business has with the individual concerned: they may be a prospective customer, a new customer, a loyal customer who offers repeat business; they may even be a customer who has left to take their business elsewhere or no longer has a requirement for our product or service.

What we actually buy is the experience, not just the product or service. The customer experience is all encompassing, and emerges from the work of many distinct disciplines: marketing, branding, product design, service design, interaction or user-experience design (as those in the digital realm often refer to it), and customer services to name a few. It also goes right to the core of the business: operations, strategy and finance all play a role in dictating the customer experience. Over the course of this book we will explore how many of these different disciplines and departments impact on the customer experience.

A skimmer's guide

The book has been written to be short and easily digestible. My aim was to write it in such a way that the reader could easily read a chapter a day on a half-hour commute, or read the book in its entirety on a transatlantic flight. That said, if you are in a real rush each chapter starts with a paragraph explaining its contents so you can decide upfront whether it's of interest; each chapter also ends with a summary of the key points that are made.

The first two chapters set the scene by explaining why the customer experience matters so much in business today, and why many businesses are struggling to make improvements; then the principles themselves are introduced in Chapter 3. To an extent each chapter can be read in isolation, but Chapters 4, 5 and 6 form a structure that the rest of the principles hang from – Chapter 4 is about understanding the customer themselves, Chapter 5 helps to pin-point their objectives, and Chapter 6 helps you to structure the customer's experience in such a way that each interaction can be worked on – so I recommend reading these in sequence, before moving on to the other principles.

Web content

A set of free downloadable worksheets to help you put the principles into action are available on my website at:

www.mattwatkinson.co.uk/worksheets

I would like to take this opportunity to thank you for buying this book, and encourage you to contact me if you have any questions or feedback about the text or the principles and how you have used them. I would also be delighted for you to share with me any great customer experiences you have had. I will keep a log of these online from which everyone can benefit. My e-mail address is:

mw@mattwatkinson.co.uk

1

Why the customer experience matters

This chapter seeks to answer one question: if the customer experience matters so much, why is it so often poor? It also sheds light on the current social and technological changes that have brought renewed interest to the area of customer experience, and what these changes mean for business in the future.

In the next village along from where I live is a great café. They provide excellent food at reasonable prices in a relaxed, friendly and comfortable environment. They know many of their customers by name and have become a social hub for our relatively small community, selling locally produced arts and crafts alongside their own produce. The owners work hard and their passion for the business is evident, not just in the quality of the food, but in the small details. There are neatly folded blankets over the chairs outside and there is always a bowl of water for customers' dogs.

They have never advertised, mainly because they've never needed to. Word spread like wildfire from the moment they opened a few years ago. I became aware of the place when I drove past one afternoon shortly after they opened and saw crowds of people outside. To get a table for breakfast requires booking in advance, and the place is usually full from the moment they open until the moment they close. Another reason they've never advertised is that the media are keen to do it for them. Last year the *Independent* newspaper named it the seventh best place in Britain to have breakfast, which is quite an achievement for a small rural café.[1] They have also been featured in the magazine of the supermarket Waitrose,[2] who themselves are renowned for their excellent customer experience.

Their success has not been to everyone's liking. The pub just down the road is virtually empty. It's dark and dingy, the food is over-priced and mediocre, the service is lacklustre and there is none of the buzzy friendly atmosphere. An air of gloom seems to hang over the place.

I booked a large table for a birthday dinner at this pub shortly after the new owner took over, thinking it would be nice to try somewhere different. At the last minute a few of my party were unable to attend, and upon my arrival I was berated by the manager for turning up with fewer people than anticipated. 'Do you know what this is going to do for our takings?!' he exclaimed. As if that wasn't bad enough, the food was dire, drinks orders were mixed up and one person's meal never even arrived.

By the end of the night I was furious and embarrassed. I said to the manager that I would come back in the morning to discuss the matter, since I was too upset to think clearly at the time. The next day the manager was apologetic. By way of compensation he offered me a weekend's stay in their hotel complete with dinner for two. Though I live close by and would never need to stay myself I accepted his offer, thinking I could pass it on to some friends who would enjoy a weekend in the countryside.

Shortly afterwards I was contacted by the owner, who had heard what had happened. He asked me to come in again to discuss things. Rather than add his own personal apology, which is what I was expecting, he told me in no uncertain terms that the offer his manager had made would not be honoured. He couldn't afford to give up a room on a weekend to a local who wasn't paying; they were barely scraping by as it was. He was not happy, and the manager had been sacked. He did however offer me alternative recompense which he felt was suitable. He went behind the bar and produced two miniature pots of homemade jam.

These two examples may seem to be at extreme ends of a spectrum, but the themes underpinning their relative successes are commonplace. The café focuses on delighting the customer in the sure knowledge that they've got a sustainable, profitable business. It's not just the food they care about, it's the whole customer experience: the service, the decor, the sense of community, and the thoughtful little touches. Customers reward them with their loyalty, and do their advertising for them.

The pub on the other hand is so focused on profit that the customer is almost seen as a necessary evil. The owner, who is often not there, is out of touch with his customers and the community. The experience is riddled with conflicting expectations, most notably between their carefully cultivated image and the somewhat disappointing reality, and those thoughtful touches that make the café so delightful are totally absent. In a nutshell, they've got their priorities back to front. The simple truth – that without customers they don't have a business at all – is lost on them.

The moral of the story is that if you focus on delighting your customers, assuming you've got your sums right, profit becomes a well earned by-product of a business that is successful in a much broader sense. You get the pleasure of knowing that you are making a positive contribution to people's lives, and customers are not going to resent you for your success. In fact, far from it, they will reward you with their loyalty and do your marketing for you.

If, however, you focus solely on maximising your profit, your decisions will bring you into direct conflict with the interests of your customer. Like the owner of the pub, you'll start cutting corners and compromising on quality to make a quick buck; you'll start over-promising and under-delivering. You'll also end up needing to do something to combat the negative feedback from customers, and replace the ones who'll never come back again: maybe reduce your prices, or spend more on advertising, both of which dig into the profits you were chasing.

Addiction to profit for profit's sake is a downward spiral, and like most forms of addiction it ends with behaviour that most ordinary people would find morally and ethically abhorrent becoming the norm. Think about the following news stories.

- Within 30 minutes of her death being announced it was reported that the price of Whitney Houston's The Ultimate Collection album was increased from £4.99 to £7.99 on the iTunes store by record label Sony Music;[3] an act described as shameless and disgusting by fans.[4]
- The UK telecoms regulator Ofcom has had to step in to 'reduce consumer harm', and remind mobile service providers of their 'tariff transparency obligations'[5] after a review found that

1.4 million mobile phone customers 'may have been affected by unexpected bill shock over the past six months'.[6] Some packages that were said to offer unlimited data actually have limits buried in the small print of the contract.

- The retail banking industry is facing a crisis of customer trust and is dogged by complaints of eye-watering charges. Consumer group Which? found that even a student studying for a PhD in maths was unable to calculate accurately the cost of an un-authorised overdraft[7] in two out of four cases. The BBC reported Santander charging an equivalent APR of 819,000 per cent on a customer going £100 overdrawn for 28 days.[8]

This state of affairs does no-one any good. Consumers have become increasingly sceptical, not just of advertising but of the corporate world in general. It's not sustainable, and it's not even in the interests of the businesses themselves. The question is, if the focus on delighting the customer is more rewarding for everyone, how then did we end up stuck in this malaise?

The Industrial Revolution

The beginning of our current situation can be found in the second half of the eighteenth century, and the arrival of machine-based manufacturing. This not only created an age where things were manufactured en masse, but also created the demand for these things through the massive economic expansion that took place. Many people could afford to have more than the bare essentials for the first time, and were keen to convey their new-found social standing through their material possessions.

For the first time, goods were no longer being produced solely by craftsmen as a direct response to a commission from a customer. In fact, it became entirely possible for goods to be produced in another part of the world. By separating those who were responsible for manufacture from the intended customer, the Industrial Revolution also gave birth to the professions of design and marketing as we currently understand them.

Mass production requires a logical, sequential process, rather than the more holistic approach used by craftsmen, and so design became critically important. Moulds and patterns needed to be made, and technical drawings were required to produce goods that were identical and, through the promise of economies of scale, affordable. Also, unlike items made by craftsmen as a response to a commission, mass produced goods were not immediately visible to potential customers. They couldn't buy them if they didn't know they existed, and so the requirement for marketing was born. Not only was design now a separate discipline from manufacture, but both design and manufacturing took place in isolation from the customer. To recover the heavy upfront costs associated with mass production, 'A more aggressive approach towards marketing and selling needed to be developed ... while production was the tail that wagged the dog.'[9]

The late nineteenth century saw the arrival of scientific management, an approach pioneered by Frederick Winslow Taylor that sought to improve efficiency and productivity in manufacturing. Taylor sought to standardise processes where possible, with the aim of increasing productivity while reducing the skill and effort required of the worker. This pushed the division of labour even further, with workers often performing highly repetitive tasks in sequence.

Taylor's approach has had a lasting impact on the enterprise, and was really the great-grandfather of what we now refer to as operations management and business process engineering. A culture dominated by efficiency, rationality and an obsession with quantitative measurement lives on in modern business, a topic I will explore in more detail in the next chapter.

Of course, neither mass production nor a predominant interest in efficiency necessarily work in opposition to the interests of the customer. The industrialised age made things that would otherwise be prohibitively expensive affordable to everyone. Our standard of living is immeasurably better owing to these developments, and modern life as we know it is the product of this Industrial Revolution. Many mass-manufactured goods have had incredible longevity and been continuing sources of delight for billions of people.

Maximising shareholder value

The consumerism that became apparent during the Industrial Revolution reached a new high in the booming economy of 1950s and 1960s America. Stoked by the golden age of advertising, image was everything, regardless of reality. Writing in *The New York Times Magazine* in 1970, Milton Friedman – Nobel Prize winner and one of the most influential economists of the twentieth century – shared his belief that 'There is one and only one social responsibility of business: to use its resources to engage in activities designed to increase its profits so long as it stays within the rules of the game, that is to say, that it engages in open and free competition, without deception or fraud.'[10]

Building on this sentiment, an article written in 1976 by two finance professors would go on to define the large-scale organisation as we see it today. The snappily titled 'Theory of the Firm, Managerial Behaviour, Agency Costs and Ownership Structure'[11] proposed that there was an inherent conflict of interest between the executives of a company (the *agents*) and the shareholders (the *principals*). The executives, although hired by the shareholders to maximise their returns, are naturally inclined to work towards their own ends, putting their interests before those of the shareholders. This theory became known as *agency theory* or the *principal–agent problem*.

The authors echoed the words of Friedman in asserting that the primary purpose of a company was to maximise shareholder returns and concluded that to solve the principal–agent problem, the goals of the executive and shareholder could be aligned by compensating the executive through shares in the company. Logic dictates that this would massively incentivise them to increase shareholder value, since it would increase their own compensation in tandem.

In his fascinating book *Fixing The Game*, Roger Martin explains how the practical application of this theory not only led to the current crises in customer relationships, but also the financial meltdowns of the last decade, from the Enron accounting scam, through the options back-dating scandals and onto the recent sub-prime mortgage debacle that plunged the world into recession.

The problem with this theory in the real world is that it shifts the CEO's attention away from the real market of customers, products and services and towards the expectation market of traders and analysts. Drawing a convincing analogy with American football, Martin explains that a CEO whose remuneration is strongly linked to share value is like sports teams being remunerated through gambling on the outcome of their own matches. It doesn't take a vivid imagination to see how that would play out: it would destroy the game and cause outrage among fans, and yet this is often how the large-scale enterprise conducts itself.

Focusing on maximising shareholder value brings the CEO into direct conflict with the interests of customers, since it is not possible to fully satisfy both the real market and the expectation market simultaneously: I can't seek to create the products or services that will most delight my customer while also trying to maximise my profit over the next three months.

Faced with a choice, the CEO's attention is on the expectation market since not only are they incentivised to do so, but it is far easier to manipulate the expectations of the stock market, or 'game the game', than it is to create genuinely brilliant experiences for the customer. It's not just the customer who loses, it's the whole company. Research published in the *Journal of Accounting and Economics* points to an alarming discovery: 'A majority of executives freely admit to sacrificing the future of their companies in order to meet the whims of the expectation market.'[12]

The inevitable consequence is that customers, employees and, ironically, even the shareholders lose out. Ethics and values evaporate and the long-term health of the organisation is sacrificed for short-term gains. 'The moral authority of business diminishes with each passing year, as customers, employees and average citizens grow increasingly appalled by the behaviour of business and the abundant greed of its leaders.'[13]

examples

Returning to the earlier themes, it is worth pointing out that although the shareholder value doctrine seems a prime culprit for the state of our current relationship with many businesses, it would not have occurred without the context created by the previous hundred years of evolution in the world of commerce. As corporations have grown, so too has the distance between the corporation and the customer. Many CEOs and senior management have little or no direct contact with customers, or many of their employees for that matter. They certainly don't know many of either by name. With the customer out of sight, it is easy for them to be out of mind, and so decisions that conflict with their interests are much easier to make. It could also be argued that the prevalent marketing and advertising culture, with its focus on image over reality, naturally lends itself to the manipulation or even exploitation of the customer. Furthermore, the Taylorist focus on economic efficiency seems a natural bed-fellow of the shareholder value doctrine: at its heart lies the maximisation of profit.

As I've said, there is nothing inherently wrong with mass production or profit, a focus on efficiency or raising awareness of products and services through marketing – few businesses can function without these things. However, when they become the tools of a leadership whose sole focus is maximising profit in the short term, they can lead to the situation we find ourselves in at present, where predatory companies exploit their customers.

Back to the customer

Roger Martin is clear on one thing – that the future of capitalism depends on shifting the focus of companies back to the customer: 'Customer delight is a more powerful objective than shareholder value … if you take care of customers, shareholders will be drawn along for a very nice ride. The opposite is simply not true: if you try to take care of shareholders, customers don't benefit, and, ironically, shareholders don't get very far either.'[14]

Not every business is of the scale where they are trading on the stock market of course, but businesses large and small have a choice whether they focus on immediate profit maximisation or on delighting the customer, as we saw with my own experience at the start of the chapter. The pub is going nowhere; the café, which opened at the height of the recent global economic crisis, is flourishing in a sector where most businesses are dropping like flies.

Although he provides a compelling argument for a shift back to the customer, Roger Martin's argument is not the only reason for renewed interest in the customer experience. Other powerful technological and social forces, which are examined below, are leaving businesses without a choice.

The information revolution

If advances in technology during the Industrial Revolution swung the balance of power towards the corporation, those of the digital revolution have swung it back towards the customer. The world wide web rapidly evolved from being a series of linked static documents into a dynamic, highly interactive platform which has changed the face of commerce and communication for ever.

E-commerce and the rise of user experience

Once people were able to buy and sell online, the importance of the user experience became apparent almost instantly. The web created an environment where there was no switching penalty to buy from one supplier or another. There was no need to walk out of a shop and across town to another one. It became the norm to type the product you want into a search engine, visit a site shown on the results, and if you couldn't get what you wanted within a few seconds, click back to the results and try another.

Companies that dominated, such as Amazon and Google, concentrated on ease of use, and everybody wanted to follow suit. Businesses started hiring usability consultants, and implementing user-centered design processes as we recognise them today.

User contributed content

A major turning point in the development of the web was when it became possible for the general public to contribute content. Discussion forums sprang up everywhere and customers were able to review products they had bought on retailers' websites. The obvious upshot of this was that consumers were able to learn from the experiences of other customers and use this as the basis for a product choice, rather than going on the carefully crafted marketing messages of the corporation. No amount of marketing can compensate for an average one-star review on Amazon. You couldn't just talk the talk anymore, you had to walk the walk.

Social media

If user contributed content started the shift of power towards the consumer, its evolution into what we now call 'social media' took things to a whole new level. In October 2010 a Dutch comedian Youp van't Hek decided to share his frustrations with his audience of 45,000 Twitter followers: 'The terror of T-Mobile is funny. For every mistake they apologise and they refer you to the customer service. Wait time 4 hours ...'[15] He had sent his son's phone in for repair and weeks had passed without successful resolution of the problem. Within half-an-hour he was contacted by a T-Mobile representative with a solution to the problem.

This sounds like a triumphant implementation of a social media strategy, where a business responds through a plethora of modern channels, but here's what happened next. Youp is even more upset that he has received preferential treatment because of his Twitter presence. He keeps up his Twitter offensive and also mentions the issue in his column in the Dutch newspaper *NRC Handelsblad*. By this point he has gained a further 10,000 followers since his first tweet on the subject, the story has caught the attention of the mass media locally and internationally[16] and T-Mobile are forced to make an official statement.[17] The story spreads to Belgium where a national radio station starts a programme inviting people to share their horror stories of dealing with customer service.

Youp keeps going, setting up an e-mail address where anybody can send in their customer service horror stories, with the view of publishing a book that will send a powerful message to large corporations that customer service really matters. The Belgian Federal Minister gets dragged into the fray, declaring the current state of customer service unacceptable. In June 2011 those companies with the biggest call centres in Belgium signed up to a charter to limit wait times to two-and-a-half minutes.[18]

There is no shortage of examples of how social media is changing the world by allowing the instantaneous formation of groups with any common interest, and giving anybody with an internet connection a giant digital megaphone to broadcast information. Social media is cited as playing a pivotal role not just in our role as consumers, but as citizens in general: it played a role in the toppling of dictators in the Arab Spring by allowing protestors to coordinate their activities, and played its part in helping Barack Obama become the first African-American President of the USA.

In his thought-provoking book *Who Cares Wins*, David Jones explains in simple terms how social media has empowered the consumer: 'Brands are defined by what consumers say to each other about them, not what a brand says to consumers.'[19] We now have open access to information which makes it impossible for a brand to tailor information to a particular audience such as investors, employees or customers, and we have the means to hold companies to account if they fail to live up to their promises. 'In today's open world it's incredibly difficult for a company to pretend it is something it's not … the key to today's successful social brand is to create the best possible reality.'[20]

Consumer design awareness

Ten years ago, when faced with confusing technology many would simply say 'I'm not a technical person.' Nowadays the consumer knows better. There are no technical and non-technical people, there are products that are well designed for their intended audience and there are those that are not, and we are now far more likely to blame the product than ourselves. This reflects a growing awareness of the role that design plays in our lives. Amazon was not the first online bookstore, Google was not the first search engine, and Ikea was not the first furniture manufacturer: their success is intrinsically linked to excellence in design.

We have a natural tendency to compare products or services with those that have set a standard rather than simply the direct competitors. I don't care whether one online grocery shopping site is better than another. If it's not as easy to use as Amazon I'll still be disappointed (which I am). My reference point for Microsoft Outlook isn't another desktop-based mail application, it's Gmail. The bar for the customer experience often isn't set by direct competitors, neither is there a clear distinction between consumer products and enterprise products like there used to be, it's set by the experiences we have in our day-to-day lives. This raises some interesting questions about the validity of competitor analysis that are covered in the next chapter.

Every man-made object that we see or touch has been designed, even if we aren't consciously aware of it. Somebody took the decisions that brought it into the world in its current form. According to designer Karim Rashid, we touch 600 such objects a day. [21] It is no surprise then that not only is our design awareness increasing, our concentration spans and patience seem to be heading in the opposite direction. We don't have the time, energy or inclination to use products or services that make our lives any more complex or stressful than they already are. These two phenomena go hand in hand. Our exposure to affordable, quality design has raised our expectations, and it's no longer enough for a product to satisfy our functional requirements; it needs to be intuitive to use, fit into our lives effortlessly and please the senses. It needs to be wrapped in a great customer experience from start to finish.

From mass production to mass customisation

Technological advances have moved the focus from straightforward mass production to mass customisation and personalisation in both the digital and physical realms. Online retailers have long had the ability to recommend items of interest to similar buyers, and we can personalise news websites so that those topics we are most interested in are given priority. We are not even scratching the service of what is possible with GPS enabled smart-phones, for showing us information that is relevant to our particular location. In the physical world we can express our individuality by choosing from thousands of options when buying a car, ordering a coffee or anything in between. Technology has done a lot to raise the bar for customer experience – we don't just want to be treated as individuals, we expect it.

Multi-channel

Perhaps the biggest challenge faced by the advances in technology isn't getting them right in isolation, it's tying them together into a consistent, holistic customer experience. The challenge is no longer simply to create a great product or service, with a good customer service offering and a useful website, it is to seamlessly join up an increasing number of different touchpoints. Many businesses find themselves having to integrate their products and services, physical shops (possibly with self-service kiosks), transactional websites, smart-phone apps, social media presence, and call centres, and not just in one country either.

Getting this kind of multi-channel experience right is an enormous challenge, but a necessary one. As we will see later, expectations are a huge aspect of the customer experience so consistency of information across the different channels is important. Pogo-sticking from the website to the call centre to the shop then back to the call centre again to solve a simple problem is infuriating, as Youp van't Hek rightly points out. We don't just want personalised customer experiences, we want them delivered in the channel that suits us best. Customer control is key to a great customer experience.

Conscientious consumption

The Industrial Revolution, design, marketing and the shareholder value doctrine are all united by the goal of economic growth through mass consumption. This model has not been without its negative consequences, as Harmut Esslinger, the founder of Frog Design, explains: 'All of those "cheap" goods that we've churned out have proven themselves to be too expensive culturally, socially, and environmentally ... The growing movement towards eco-capitalism isn't an exercise in "do-goodism". It's driven by self-preservation.'[22]

There has never been greater attention paid to the social and environmental cost of our consumption, and for a growing number of consumers the socio-environmental impact of a product is another rationale to throw into the mix when making a purchasing decision. While it is certainly not the only rationale, choosing organic food, fair-trade coffee, recycled and recyclable products, or a hybrid car are obvious ways that consumers are demonstrating their growing concerns.

In *Who Cares Wins*, David Jones argues that social media and corporate social responsibility are intrinsically linked, since social media has enabled the consumer to hold businesses to account. He starts by describing the three ages of the socially responsible business. The first, *The Age of Image (1990–2000)*, was all about brands altering their outward appearance rather than making any real change to how things were done. It was about appearing to be green or ethical rather than actually doing it. The second, *The Age of Advantage (2000–2010)*, was when businesses began to see genuine social responsibility as a source of competitive advantage. He concludes that we are now living in the third age, *The Age of Damage*, where businesses that are not socially responsible will be damaged as a result.[23]

The increasing importance of corporate social responsibility perfectly illustrates how some of the factors we've already examined are playing out in the marketplace. A move away from Friedman's absolute focus on profit is not just a response to growing customer outrage about service standards, it's recognition that the social and environmental consequences of this mercenary approach are unacceptable. Social media has empowered the consumer to hold these businesses to account if they fail to deliver either on their responsibilities to society or on their obligations to their customers.

Finally, there is growing awareness that the environmental problems we face are as much a design issue as anything. So much of the waste that we experience is down to poor design: planned obsolescence, wildly excessive packaging, or products that break but end up in the landfill because they can't be economically repaired. As we will see later in the book, reflecting the personal values of the customer through a product or service is fundamental to a great customer experience.

(R)evolution

What we are experiencing is part evolution part revolution. Technology is the great propeller of social change as it always has been, and emerging 'green-blooded' entrepreneurs are helping capitalism evolve in a more socially and environmentally responsible direction. Yet from the customer's point of view this is a revolution in one sense of the word, since we now find the world of business turning back towards the customer. The gap between businesses and the customers they serve is being narrowed by social media: there is greater collaboration and a more bilateral dialogue than there has been for a long time. The power of traditional marketing has been curbed by user contributed content, and there is less and less choice but to commit fully to delighting the customer to stay in business.

The fact remains that this approach has always been the best way for businesses large or small to succeed in the long term. As management pedagogue Peter F. Drucker said in 1955, 'The purpose of a business is to create and keep a customer.'[24] What we are experiencing is not a new discovery, it's a renewal of interest brought about by a confluence of technological and social change, set against a backdrop of political and economic upheaval.

A great customer experience is good for business, and always has been – we reward those that provide them with loyalty, repeat business, and by doing their marketing for them – telling friends, family and colleagues about their products and services.

Business leaders have always been quick to extol the virtues of concentrating on the customer. Office walls and mission statements have always been covered with rhetoric: 'Every customer counts' ... 'Go the extra mile for the customer' ... 'We need to be customer obsessed!' The difference is that now they actually have to do it, and those that do are reaping the benefits.

In May 2011 a three-year-old girl wrote to UK supermarket Sainsbury's, saying that one of their products, 'tiger bread', should be re-named: 'Why is tiger bread called tiger bread? It should be called giraffe bread. Love from Lily Robinson age 3 and ½.' She received a reply from a customer service agent that said, 'I think renaming tiger bread giraffe bread is a brilliant idea – it looks much more like the blotches on a giraffe than the stripes on a tiger, doesn't it? It is called tiger bread because the first baker who made it a l-o-o-o-ng time ago thought it looked stripey like a tiger. Maybe they were a bit silly.' The letter was signed 'Chris King (age 27 and ⅓)'.[25]

I first heard about this story when it appeared on my own Facebook feed. It has been seen by hundreds of thousands of people and covered by BBC News. Most of the comments were hugely positive towards Chris King and the Sainsbury's brand. A couple of examples: 'That's what I call good customer service!' ... 'Simple gestures like this can and do generate immense goodwill for the brand, yet is still so rare' ... 'If there were more Chris Kings working, bad customer service would be a thing of the past!' Sainsbury's were quick to capitalise on the coverage, promptly renaming the bread 'giraffe bread'. No doubt thousands of people went to their websites and stores to see if they had in fact renamed the bread.

The topic of social media seems to have put marketers and public relations professionals in a bind. On the one hand they are scared stiff of the damage a concerted social media campaign against their brand could do, but on the other hand find the potential opportunities irresistible. There does seem to be one simple option: if you want your customers to tweet positive things about you, focus on creating a great customer experience, and like the example from Sainsbury's, the customers will do the rest for you. By contrast, those businesses that have lost touch with the customers they serve will be rich pickings for entrepreneurs who put the customer experience at the heart of their business. It's not *if*, it's *when*.

Summary

- Create a great customer experience and profit will be a happy by-product of a successful business in a much broader sense.

- A blinkered focus on profit maximisation brings you into direct conflict with the interests of your customers.

- The Industrial Revolution that led to mass production and the division of labour brought separation between the manufacturer and the customer. Over time as companies grew and grew, so did the rift with the customer.

- Tying executive compensation to share price has shifted the leadership's attention away from the customer and towards the stock market, a contributing factor to the current malaise.

- Social media is starting to empower the consumer, providing a largely unregulated, democratic means to hold businesses to account for disappointing or dishonest behaviour.

- Personalisation and customisation are becoming the norm, raising customer expectations.

- The profusion of new digital touchpoints – smart-phones, kiosks, websites – has created headaches for businesses that now need to join them up into consistent experiences.

- There is greater awareness and appreciation of good design. If we cannot work a product we are more likely to blame the design of the product than ourselves.

- There is increasing interest in the social responsibility of businesses as we grow more conscious of the social and environmental impact of our consumption.

- Businesses now have little choice but to concentrate on delighting the customer to stay in business.

2

Why customer experiences aren't improving

This chapter explains why efforts to improve the customer experience often don't deliver the results that are hoped for. It explores some of the issues typically present in large organisations that often stand in the way of creating a great customer experience.

Getting it wrong

Despite widespread understanding that the customer experience is critically important, as consumers we are still often frustrated and disappointed. Products are too complex to use, small print leaves us feeling cheated, adverts bear little resemblance to reality, customer service is often rude. Examples of poor customer experiences are a daily occurrence for most of us. Genuinely brilliant ones are still incredibly rare, despite the renewed interest in this area.

Why is this? It's usually not for a lack of trying. It's not a budgetary issue either – some companies spend millions on market research, user testing and customer care programmes. It's not that the people involved aren't intelligent or talented. There are plenty of smart people who 'get it'. What's going on?

While no two companies are the same, there are a few causes that are worth exploring in more detail. They are drawn from my experience working with medium and large businesses, although you may find they are equally applicable to smaller ones too.

The Vulcan death grip

The recent *Star Trek* movie directed by J.J. Abrams follows the early part of the relationship between the two lead characters. One, the human James T. Kirk is hot-headed and emotional; the other is Spock, a Vulcan, who suppresses all emotion, seeking to live by only rational and logical thought. Needless to say, they don't exactly see eye-to-eye.

Businesses primarily follow the Vulcan model, seeing their enterprise as a supremely rational endeavour. They check their normal lives in at the door in the name of Spock-like professionalism. As the doyen of design Don Norman concludes, 'Business has come to be ruled by logical, rational decision makers ... with no room for emotion. Pity!'[1]

In our role as consumers we couldn't be less Vulcan. We are often impulsive, basing purchasing decisions solely on emotions, hunches or intuition. Clearly the more in touch a business is with our emotional wants and needs, the more its products or services will resonate with us.

At the end of the movie, while Kirk is captain, Spock serves as his first officer on the *Enterprise,* giving them the best of both worlds. This should serve as an excellent model for businesses to emulate when making decisions: a total understanding of the consumer – their thoughts, feelings and experiential requirements – balanced by rigorous analysis and rational processes. In most cases, however, the rational and analytical have become a substitute for a more empathic, human understanding rather than the other side of the same coin. Here are two common ways in which this phenomenon manifests itself.

Measurebating

Ken Rockwell coined the term 'Measurebator' to describe a type of photographer who is more interested in the theoretical performance of a camera than whether it takes great photos or not. 'These folks have analysis paralysis and never accomplish anything,' he says. 'These people worry so much about trying to put numerical ratings on things that they are completely oblivious to the fact that cameras or test charts have nothing to do with the spirit of an image.'[2]

The office Vulcans have taken measurebating to its zenith, using a variety of tools to analyse competitors, model customer segments and report on market activity. Unfortunately, these models are only representative of reality; they aren't reality itself.

As Dev Patnaik explains in *Wired to Care*, 'Companies have become so dependent on models that many organisations have started to lose touch with reality. Without personal connection to the people they serve, companies lack the context, immediacy, or experience they need to make good decisions. Far too many leaders make critical decisions without any personal feel for the territory.'[3]

When working on website projects I've often been asked to make the phone number for customer services less prominent. 'We have a strategic objective to reduce the traffic to our call centres,' they say. 'It's about cost reduction.' This demonstrates a tendency for people to advocate decisions that can degrade the customer experience when numbers and analytics work against empathy.

Numbers and calculations can rob people of their humanity with truly harrowing consequences. In his deeply thought-provoking paper 'Accounting in the Service of the Holocaust', Warwick Funnel argues that 'Accounting numbers were substituted for qualitative attributes of individuals thereby denying them their humanity and individuality … (Accounting) was not only a means of expediting the annihilation of the Jews but was also one of the means by which people who had no direct involvement in the murder of millions of Jews were able to divorce themselves from the objectives and consequences of their work.'[4] When people are reduced to numbers, it's hard to see them as people anymore.

Another form of measurebating is the return on investment calculation that is typically required as part of a business case to get funding for a project. It's a topic that grates on many in the design world, since it is almost impossible to translate something that is qualitative into something quantitative, especially when the experience is inseparable from the functionality that delivers it. I remember one client trying to prepare a business case for a new feature that would show a product on the website in each of the different colours that were available. The question was, how much would this increase conversion from people browsing the page to actually buying? Would it increase the 'basket value' of people shopping on the site? It's impossible to measure in isolation since there are so many other variables that require consideration – the product itself, seasonal variance, other improvements to the site that are launched simultaneously to name but a few.

Drag racing

Unlike discrete elements of the customer experience, there are many aspects of a business that are easy to measure: how many people you have performing a task, how much they are paid, or how long a particular process takes. Since Taylor's invention of scientific management in the late nineteenth century, which I mentioned in the previous chapter, the optimisation and standardisation of processes to reduce waste and maximise efficiency has dominated the focus of many organisations. The easier something is to measure, the more of a target it becomes. Computers and machinery are mercilessly replacing humans, and consulting firms make good money from finding cost savings, especially in a recession.

Efficiency has an appeal to both businesses and their customers. As customers we hate waiting around for things to happen, and operating more efficiently can save a business money. As a designer I have a particular fondness for things that operate with wonderful economy, or are cleverly packaged to minimise waste.

You can, however, have too much of a good thing. Nowadays it's not just the pace of business that is accelerating, it's the pace of change. Flexibility is as important as speed when expectations can change at the drop of a hat. Unfortunately, in their zeal for efficiency, some have engineered out all the slack they can from their businesses at the expense of agility. As Tom DeMarco puts it in his book *Slack*, 'An organisation that can accelerate but not change direction is like a car that can speed up but not steer. In the short run it makes a lot of progress in whatever direction it happens to be going. In the long run, it's just another road wreck.'[5]

The consequences for customer experience can be severe: hyper-efficient companies are usually unable to respond to changes in customer expectations, and any customer issue that does not fit neatly into the optimised solution cannot be dealt with satisfactorily. Few things are more infuriating than calling customer services just to go through eight different menu options unsure of what to choose, when all you want to do is speak to someone about an urgent problem. The automated supermarket till may require fewer people to work in the shop in theory, but the machine is unable to cope with an unexpected item in the bagging area.

Attack of the clones

Measurebators also find competitor analysis irresistible. They are frequently found compiling spreadsheets that list each of the features and functions of every product on the market so that they can position their own products or services with absolute precision.

This has two unfortunate side effects. The first is that competition becomes a contest of one-up-manship: products gain more megapixels, features and functions, which compromises the experience by making the thing more and more difficult to use. It also means you are always one step behind the people you are benchmarking against. As David Heinemeier Hansson and Jason Fried, authors of *Rework,* put it, 'When you get suckered into an arms race you wind up in a never-ending battle that costs you massive amounts of money, time and drive. And it forces you to constantly be on the defensive, too. Defensive companies can't think ahead; they can only think behind. They don't lead; they follow.'[6]

The other inevitable side effect is that imitation is almost inevitable when you measure yourself against the competition in this way. This goes some way to explaining why most products on sale bear a remarkable resemblance to the original innovator in the field.

I want it yesterday

When designers are forced to work to unrealistic timescales, two things tend to happen. The first is that they abandon any kind of sensible structured approach, and then they look for things to copy. I feel for these guys, I really do. They usually don't have the clout to tell their boss's boss where to go. The same is true in agencies: if the client wants it, they'll bend over forward to do it on time. It's become an epidemic that means offerings get rushed to market without thorough design or testing, with obvious consequences. A good customer experience requires careful thought and consideration of the finest details. It is not something that can be rushed.

Even if a business commits to a well-structured customer experience improvement programme they often find they are hamstrung by legacy technology that is itself the product of the hurry-up mantra. Years of patches, bodges and duct-tape in the technology that runs the company can make the experience that businesses desire so much an impossibility. They need to re-platform first and then the whole cycle starts again because they need the new tech yesterday.

If you need to be in another country for a morning meeting, it's no good getting on a late plane and telling the pilot to just fly faster. If you want it sooner, you need to start earlier, and that means looking further into the future. Therein lies the rub. Too much of what businesses undertake is driven by short-term thinking. A poor customer experience is often symptomatic of a bigger problem: a lack of vision at the top or a programme structured around quarterly profit statements.

It's a recognised problem. In January 2012 *Wired* magazine ran a feature entitled '25 big ideas for 2012', and on that list in among the various bleeding-edge advancements in technology was an article titled 'Here for the Long Haul – Corporate Long-Termism'. The author, David Rowan, explains how business juggernauts including SoftBank, IBM and Unilever have 'shied away from short-term shareholder concerns'[7] and are looking towards the long term. They aren't the only ones.

In *Fixing the Game*, which I mentioned in the last chapter, Roger Martin explains how we 'must shift the focus of companies back to the customer and away from shareholder value',[8] citing Johnson & Johnson, Proctor & Gamble and Apple as companies which are getting it right. The message is clear. If you focus on taking care of your customers your shareholders will benefit too, if you try the opposite nobody does, but who does our CEO task with improving the customer experience? The answer is not a straightforward one.

The empty chair[9]

In the business that you work for, who is responsible or indeed accountable for the customer experience? The only time I've ever known for sure is when it has been me, and even then I've often felt like I'm not. If you can't immediately answer with at least one person's name, there is a strong likelihood that your customer experience is suffering as a result.

Look at the board of directors of a large business, and there tend to be a few standard positions that are filled: CEO for strategy and leadership; CFO for finance and accounting; COO takes care of operations; CTO for technology; CMO is in charge of marketing. Who then is responsible for the customer experience? Where is the CXO? The Chief Experience Officer. If no single person is explicitly responsible for the customer experience, and no single person is held accountable if it's not right, we're in a pickle right from the start.

Getting the customer experience right necessarily involves coordination of almost every part of the business, but if no one person is unambiguously calling the shots then failure is almost inevitable. I've experienced this first-hand. Words like 'ownership' and 'sponsorship' start getting thrown around and the whole thing descends into a political bunfight as each stakeholder group seeks to grab as much control as they can. Progress internally becomes agonisingly slow, whoever has the most political sway or the deepest pockets gets their way, and designers either quit or become more concerned with keeping stakeholders happy than with creating something great. The voice of the customer gets lost in the mêlée, and nothing improves.

Apple have taken the opposite approach. Steve Jobs is quoted in his biography by Walter Isaacson as saying that design chief Jonathan Ive 'has more operational power than anyone else at Apple except me. There's no one who can tell him what to do or to butt out. That's the way I set it up.'[10] This may go some way to explaining why the design of their products appears to have such purity. By contrast, of the companies that I've consulted for in the last seven years, not one has had design or customer experience represented at board level, yet almost all of them have referenced Apple as the gold standard to which they aspire.

Putting the politics aside, without top-level representation, decisions that affect the customer experience end up being made unwittingly. Quality and expectations start to vary depending on which department was responsible, and what *their* goals and objectives are. This leads to wild inconsistencies throughout the customer journey that can make it hard for customers to know what to expect. When a product or service is mis-sold by salespeople hungry to meet their targets, it's usually customer services that pick up the pieces and the whole brand ends up tarnished. Rarely is the root source of the problem held to account in such situations.

The Net Promoter Score

These problems are well understood and many organisations are taking steps to solve them. One approach that goes some way towards resolving these issues is the Net Promoter Score ('NPS'), a system that seeks to quantify how well a business is managing its relationships with customers. The creator of the system, Fred Reichheld, is quick to point out a fundamental problem with an over-emphasis on financial analysis by introducing a distinction between bad profits and good profits.[11]

Bad profits, he explains, are earned in ways that we as customers generally find abhorrent: hidden charges in the small print, contracts that lock you in, confusing pricing, and poor customer service among others. Good profits, on the other hand, come from delighting the customer so they come back for more and enthusiastically tell their friends and family about their experiences.

The problem as Reichheld sees it is that accounting metrics are unable to distinguish between the two sources of profit, and companies easily become hooked on bad profits: 'This addiction to bad profits demotivates employees, diminishes the chances for true growth, and accelerates a destructive spiral. Customers resent bad profits – and investors should, too, because bad profits undermine a company's prospects.'[12]

His solution, which was first published in the *Harvard Business Review* in late 2003, is simple, yet powerful. It relies on categorising customers based on their answers to the following questions:

On a zero to ten scale, how likely is it that you would recommend us (or this product/service/brand) to a friend or colleague?

Followed by:

What is the primary reason for your score?

Promoters are people who responded with a nine or ten. These are loyal customers who share their positive experiences with those around them. They tend to spend more and are enthusiastic about the brand, product or service.

Passives are those who gave a seven or eight score. These are unlikely to recommend the brand and if they do it's with caveats and little enthusiasm. They would most probably leave if a competitor offering was tempting enough. Businesses should aim to turn these people into promoters.

Detractors are any score of six or below. These are the guys you see who have had a bad experience and bad-mouth the company. Their problems need to be taken seriously.

To arrive at the Net Promoter Score you simply take the percentage of customers who are promoters and subtract the percentage that are detractors.[13]

Advocates of NPS explain how it provides them with insights that are actionable, and critically takes something that was once deemed too intangible to measure accurately and turns it into something quantifiable. They also find that their Net Promoter Score 'ties directly to revenue growth'[14] and that, in fact, the value of a promoter or detractor can be quantified. This is a great solution because it fits perfectly with the corporation's love of measuring things, and also provides grounds for investing in the customer experience that appeals to even the most ardent measurebator.

It is no surprise that there are plenty of promoters for the net promoter system; it has, after all, enabled many businesses to become more customer-centric. But what happens after we discover our score, and then need to make some changes? We need some mechanism for turning our findings into tangible improvements in our customer experience. Knowing the score and having a target can't do it for us. That's where this book comes in, to provide you with the toolkit you need to improve your customer experience. Let's get started.

Summary

- A bias towards rationalism and quantitative analysis cannot substitute an empathic feel for what will delight the customer.

- Reducing decision making to a numbers game de-humanises the customer. Since many experiential factors do not naturally lend themselves to the traditional return on investment calculation they are often overlooked.

- Hyper-efficiency leaves businesses unable to respond to changes in customer expectations.

- Competitor analysis leads to imitation. Products and services become derivative from the market leaders, who pull even further ahead.

- Short termism leads to shaky technology foundations that put a strait-jacket on the customer experience. It also leads to short-cuts in improvement projects that compromise the quality of their output.

- Accountability and responsibility need to be clear if the customer experience is to improve. In most cases there are neither at board level, making the whole topic a political nightmare.

- The Net Promoter Score has brought with it a useful measure of the quality of a customer experience which strongly correlates to growth, but it can't make the improvements for you.

3

The ten principles behind great customer experiences

This chapter introduces the ten principles behind great customer experiences, and highlights the key benefits to using a principle based approach to both identifying problems and making improvements. The chapter concludes with some guidelines for their usage.

1 **Great customer experiences strongly reflect the customer's identity**

   Our beliefs and values play a decisive role in our behaviour as customers. Those experiences that reinforce our self-image and resonate with our personal values leave us feeling good about our decisions, while those brands that clearly stand for something engender much stronger loyalty. This is essential to getting the experience right at a *brand level*.

2 **Great customer experiences satisfy our higher objectives**

   In a movie, what makes each character interesting are the objectives hidden beneath what they say or do. Customers are no different: wants and needs are derivative, it is satisfying the higher objective behind them that is the foundation on which great experiences are built. This is fundamental to getting the experience right at a *product or service level*.

3 **Great customer experiences leave nothing to chance**

   To create consistent, smooth customer journeys, every interaction needs to be considered, planned and designed. There is no detail that is too small to consider. This is the starting point for getting the experience right at an *interaction level*.

4 **Great customer experiences set and then meet expectations**

   Existing expectations, learnt behaviours and associations are the criteria that customers use to judge an experience from the beginning. Great customer experiences explicitly consider these factors, and exceed expectations where desirable.

5 Great customer experiences are effortless

Interactions that put the onus on the customer, soaking up their time and energy, are quickly put off or replaced with those that are less demanding. Few things generate more goodwill and repeat business than being effortless to deal with.

6 Great customer experiences are stress free

We all instinctively avoid stressful situations. Customer experiences that eliminate confusion, uncertainty and anxiety reap the rewards, generating a competitive advantage, loyalty and a peerless brand image.

7 Great customer experiences indulge the senses

From delicious food to relaxing music or a beautiful painting, we all actively seek sensory pleasure. Customer experiences that delight the senses win our hearts and have us coming back for more.

8 Great customer experiences are socially engaging

The importance of cultivating personal relationships with customers cannot be over-stated: we more readily buy from a friend than a stranger. However, our position within a social group is also a powerful and private motivator. Those experiences that elevate our status are often the most highly valued.

9 Great customer experiences put the customer in control

Control is fundamentally important to us: we want to do things in our own time and in our own way, and we take exception to those encounters that force us to jump through hoops. By contrast, we appreciate experiences that are flexible, accommodating and leave us feeling in control.

10 Great customer experiences consider the emotions

We are all slaves to our emotions, yet most see their customers from a purely rational perspective. Evaluating the emotional aspect of an experience brings often unconsidered issues to the surface and opens up new ways to delight the customer.

Why use principles?

There are many practical benefits that come from using these simple principles to guide your decision making and help structure your thinking. Here are the key ones:

- Principles are easy to understand
- Principles are quick and efficient
- Principles are scalable
- Principles are flexible
- Principles can be de-centralised
- Principles foster innovation
- Principles complement existing ways of working
- Principles last longer than ideas
- Principles create deeper understanding

PRINCIPLES ARE EASY TO UNDERSTAND

Convoluted processes and complex data analysis might look clever, but unless an approach can be quickly and easily understood – by those who will use it and other stakeholders too – implementation is an uphill struggle. By contrast, the principles of customer experience in this book are easy to understand, so can be put straight to work, by anyone.

PRINCIPLES ARE QUICK AND EFFICIENT

Using principles to guide you reduces your dependency on inspiration and imitation, and they can help you get through the wall when you know something just isn't right with your solution. They can also bring structure to research and testing. This means less time is wasted in subjective debates, pixel pushing and aimless experimenting in the hope of arriving at something that feels right.

PRINCIPLES ARE SCALABLE

Every business, large or small, has a customer experience, and yet the issues they face and the approaches they take to solve them will vary depending on the scale of the enterprise. A small business may know their customers as individuals; a global retailer may have cultural differences to contend with in different countries. These principles can help whatever the size of the business, since they are based on how the brain works: something common to every customer.

PRINCIPLES ARE FLEXIBLE

Bach, Mozart and Jimi Hendrix all understood the theory of music, but this didn't stop them creating their own distinctive styles or producing thousands of unique compositions. The same goes for the psychological principles behind customer experiences: they can be interpreted and applied in infinite ways, supporting rather than constraining creativity. Competitor analysis and benchmarking has the opposite effect. It narrows the frame of reference to the point where the only visible solution is that of the market leader.

PRINCIPLES CAN BE DE-CENTRALISED

Not every facet of the customer experience can be controlled centrally – the quality of the experience is often in the hands of individual front-line staff, either manning the phones in customer services, or in a store. In situations where the customer has an unusual query or problem that needs resolving, the usual response is to defer to the judgement of a supervisor, or utter some kind of meaningless 'computer says no' answer. It doesn't have to be this way – any business could give its front-line staff a set of customer-experience guidelines to follow as part of their training. This would not only make their jobs more rewarding by giving them a little more autonomy, but would also tune them into noticing opportunities and issues. Everybody wins. These principles can help with this.

PRINCIPLES FOSTER INNOVATION

In the creative thinking manual *Thinkertoys*, author Michael Michalko explains that 'By changing your perspective, you expand your possibilities until you see something you were unable to see before ... This new and different way of seeing things will lead you to new ideas and insights.'[1] These principles allow you to do exactly that, by giving ten different perspectives to frame the customer experience, rather than just asking 'Is it usable?' or 'Did the customer complete the task?' Using the different principles in this book to frame problems can lead to innovations by helping you think about the experience differently.

PRINCIPLES COMPLEMENT EXISTING WAYS OF WORKING

Most businesses of scale have established workflows for improving their customer experience, whether it be a user-centered design process for enhancing their website, or a partnership with a research company that helps them keep track of trends. A great thing about using these principles is that they work with existing approaches rather than trying to replace them. They add another layer of intelligence to what already exists and may already be giving great results.

By contrast, trying to embed a new process in an organisation can be fraught with difficulties. In a way, since these principles are more about structuring your thinking, they don't even really need implementation at all. You can just use them and let the results do the talking. This is exactly how I started out with them. I used them in my day-to-day design work, and it wasn't long before people took note.

PRINCIPLES LAST LONGER THAN IDEAS

Good ideas can become toxic over time. As the world turns, expectations and technology change, and what was once a brilliant solution can start to do more harm than good. Principles on the other hand tend to have a long shelf life. Using them as a starting point can help you see the wood for the trees.

PRINCIPLES CREATE DEEPER UNDERSTANDING

Prescriptive solutions – in case of x do y – can only get you so far. To really understand the problems and opportunities we are presented with, we need to trace things back to their roots.

One of the most powerful problem solving techniques in the Japanese continuous improvement philosophy *Kaizen* is Toyota's 'Five Why's Analysis', which can be used to trace a problem back to a root cause. There is a puddle of oil on the shopfloor. Why? Because the machine is leaking oil. Why? Because the gasket has deteriorated. Why? Because we bought gaskets made of inferior material. Why? Because we got a good price. Why? Because purchasing agents are evaluated on short-term cost savings achieved. The solution, then, is to change the evaluation policy for service agents.[2]

This is a brilliant approach to problem solving and truly helps to develop a deep understanding. I followed this approach during the course of my research for this book and in my design practice, and have found that in the vast majority of cases problems can be traced back to the principles I propose here. Using them will help you to develop a deeper understanding of what makes a great customer experience.

Before we get started

The rest of the text explores the ten principles in detail, covering their theoretical foundations and how they can be used in practice, supported by examples. I hope that by the time you've finished you will never think about customer experiences in the same way, whichever side of the office wall you are sitting on. As a fun exercise, whenever you have an especially good or bad customer experience, think about which of the ten principles are at work. You'll quickly internalise them and realise how they play out in practice.

I believe these principles are collectively exhaustive – that there isn't a facet of the customer experience that isn't covered by at least one of them. However, they are not mutually exclusive, and there are some topics that could appear under more than one principle.

As an example, the subject of human error could easily fall under effort, since the more errors a customer makes the more re-working there is; or it could fall under stress, since making mistakes can also undermine a customer's confidence and leave them worrying about whether they have performed a task correctly. I've followed a simple approach to resolving this, which is to try to make the chapters short enough that one can be read per day on a short commute. Where topics overlap I've split them up to make them more easily digestible, and where appropriate I've cross-referenced them.

Not all of the principles apply equally to every part of every experience. There are normally one or two that come to the fore in any given situation, like 'the customer was expecting something else' or 'the task just takes too long'. This is great for solving the most obvious problems, but you will also find that framing a task using the other principles generates previously unconsidered ideas and new opportunities.

Finally, as I will demonstrate through examples, these principles are at work regardless of the price point or sector. If you have a customer, these principles will work. Creating a great customer experience isn't the sole preserve of luxury brands, expensive products and services, or big budget projects. Anyone can do it.

Summary

- There are ten principles that can be used to identify opportunities to improve the customer experience.

- These principles are universal: they apply to products and services, and to businesses of any size, in any sector.

- These principles are easy to understand and complement existing ways of working, making them easy to implement.

- Using these principles to structure your thinking and guide your decision making will help you come up with better ideas in less time, and will reduce your dependency on inspiration and imitation.

- The rest of the book shows you how to put these principles to work.

Great customer experiences strongly reflect the customer's identity

Our beliefs and values play a decisive role in our behaviour as customers and those experiences that reinforce our self-image and resonate with our personal values leave us feeling good about our decisions, while those brands that clearly stand for something engender much stronger loyalty. This chapter will show you where our beliefs and values come from, how they drive consumption and how you can make sure that the experience accurately reflects the customer's identity. This is how to get the experience right at a brand level.

People do not build their beliefs on a foundation of reason. They begin with certain beliefs, then find reasons to justify them. EUGENE P. WIGNER

Introduction

In August 2011 there was widespread rioting and looting in some English cities. Many of us sat glued to the television as the police struggled to control the chaos. Shopkeepers saw their businesses go up in flames. Millions of pounds worth of public and private property was destroyed. The looters were targeting plasma screen television sets, sportswear and mobile phones. It seems that if you can walk down the high street and take anything, you take what you want not what you need.

Understanding consumption

The starting point for creating a great customer experience is not looking at what people 'need', because most people's needs are met. We actually need very little. We operate in a world of wants, not needs. The question is, why do people want one thing over another? To build an appealing customer experience we need to start by understanding the mechanics of consumption.

The object value system

The French philosopher Jean Baudrillard explored the concepts of consumerism and value in detail, concluding that there are four sources of value for an object:

- *Use value* is the function or utility of an object – a pencil draws, a refrigerator cools

- *Exchange value* is the economic or market value – a pig is worth two sheep, a pen is worth two pounds

- *Symbolic value* is the value conferred on an object as a symbol of a relationship between two people – a gift, a wedding ring, or a graduation present

- *Sign value* is the value of the object in relation to other similar objects, and what it says about the owner in a social context – a Mont Blanc pen signifies different values, status and taste to a Bic

Baudrillard argued that consumption is driven by the *sign value* of the object – what it says about the consumer – and this determines the *exchange value* – what it's worth.[1] Consumption is driven not by any kind of objective need, but as a means to convey our beliefs, values and self-image. An official report into the London riots identified 'the desire for high-profile brands'[2] as a significant factor. They were looting for sign value.

Connoisseurship

If this sign value is what drives consumption, then it should follow that the more visible or obvious the signs are the better, but we see almost exactly the opposite in practice. Some people take great delight in owning 'Q cars' which are enormously powerful but look ordinary. Anyone with money can buy a diamond encrusted Rolex to display their wealth, but it takes a true connoisseur to recognise a vintage 'Double-Red' Sea Dweller ($50,000+). As William Whyte puts it in *The Organisation Man*, 'the more exquisite distinctions are, the more important they become'.[3]

This doesn't just apply to luxury brands. Every social group however small has such cues, and any purchase that has a sign value is a form of consumption. My father, who has a deep appreciation for engineering, has a house stuffed full of vintage clocks. He certainly isn't trying to impress anyone with them, in fact, unless you go to his house, you'll never know he has them. This is perhaps the most important point about sign value. The brands we buy and the products we own tell a story, and the audience for that story is most often *ourselves*. It is our personal beliefs and values that drive our consumption, but where do these come from and why do they matter so much?

The gyroscope and the radar

One explanation for the source of our beliefs and values is offered by David Reisman, whose hugely influential book *The Lonely Crowd* was published in 1961. The author explores the relationship between social character and society, proposing three distinct types.

In a *tradition-directed* society, conformity reflects an individual's 'age grade, clan or caste'[4] and important relationships are 'controlled by careful and rigid etiquette'[5] and rituals that have existed for centuries.

In an *inner-directed* society, individuals are not simply controlled by behavioural conformity, but by an inner 'gyroscope'[6] set early in their lives by parents and authorities that keeps them on track. An inner-directed individual can choose to pursue far more courses than the tradition-directed one – wealth, knowledge, power or fame among others – since they are directed by their character rather than restricted by the traditions of the day.

The *other-directed* individual is guided by their contemporaries, through 'exceptional sensitivity to the actions and wishes of others'.[7] Their chief aim is to be liked by their social group. Their 'control equipment, instead of being like a gyroscope, is like a radar'.[8]

To an extent, every individual is a blend of these three character types – tradition-directed, inner-directed and other-directed – and each has a role to play in establishing our values and beliefs. Resolving the tension between inner and other direction remains a huge source of value to the anxious modern consumer. We want at once to be individuals but also to belong to a group. Few things would ruin a party for one of my female friends like wearing the same dress as another guest, even though they would want to be seen as similarly fashionable.

To me, Reisman's most interesting observation is that as society has become increasingly governed by consumption there has been a shift towards *other-directedness*.[9] As consumer culture has developed we have become more adept at reading and using this sign value to communicate our identities. The tutor is now no longer the parents, but the peer group and the media, who direct us.

Reisman's observations were eerily prescient. He explains how the other-directed man suffers an 'inability to know what he wants, whilst being pre-occupied with what he likes'[10] and that his heroes are the captains of the consumer industries 'actors, artists, entertainers' whose consumption habits take centre stage: 'the heroes dress, food, women and recreation are emphasised'.[11] This is exactly the state of consumer culture today, as one glance down the shelves at the newsagent will confirm.

The other-directed business

It is not only consumers who have shifted towards other-directedness and ended up struggling: businesses have too. The dominant obsession with market intelligence, competitor analysis and customer research is all about developing a more powerful radar, and the endless hand-wringing and strategising over social media betrays the kind of anxieties that are most often found in those eager for the approval of others.

By contrast, we most admire those businesses with a strong inner direction – a clear set of values, integrity and sense of purpose – and tend to lionise celebrity CEOs who bring that ethos to life. Telecoms companies, banks, insurance providers, airlines and energy suppliers find themselves tyrannised by price comparison websites because there is simply no other way of choosing between them. Customers churn between suppliers to find the best deal, not because we are all extremely price sensitive, but because there is nothing to be loyal to.

I hold Ryanair in far higher esteem than many other carriers because at least I don't need to check their mission statement to know what they are about: safety, the lowest possible prices, and arriving on time. It may not be the most luxurious experience flying with them, but we know what we are getting ourselves into. I've flown extensively for work and leisure and the lack of differentiation between most carriers is criminal. Rather than building a more powerful radar, what these businesses should be doing is getting their gyroscope spinning. Our beliefs and values play a decisive role in our behaviour as customers, and those experiences that reinforce our self-image appeal to us on a deeper level. The rest of this chapter explores how this insight can be put into practice.

Customer profiling #1 – brand, function and price

To create an offering that appeals to the customer, we need to know as much about that customer as possible, and so most businesses try to capture this information in customer profiles of one sort or another. There is another reason for this – there is often more than one distinctive customer group, so we need to know not just how customers are similar but also how they are different. Baudrillard's object value system provides a good place to start. Get a piece of paper and a pen and answer these questions:

- *Use value* – Do all our customers want a product that performs the same function? What are these functions?
- *Exchange value* – Do all our customers have the same budget or willingness to pay? What are these price points?
- *Sign value* – Do all our customers want to say the same things about themselves? What exactly is the message?

Being able to accurately answer these questions alone will stand you head and shoulders above most, and will give you a solid starting point for understanding how your customers differ at the highest level.

Consider what the brand should say about the customer

If sign value is what drives consumption, then we need to think carefully about what the brand, product or service says about the consumer. Write down answers to the following questions:

1 Does your customer see themselves as more inner- or other-directed?
2 Does the brand reflect membership of a social group or community?
3 To what extent does your intended customer want to emphasise their individuality?
4 Think of the product as an avatar for the customer – what does it say about them?
5 Who do the signs tell the story to – themselves, other people or both?
6 Who should be able to read these signs?

7 Think about connoisseurship – how subtle do the signs need to be?

8 Does the brand confer a particular status on the customer?

9 Does the customer have a unique set of values that they are expressing through the brand, or are other rationales more important?

10 Finally, if your brand is the answer, what is the question? (This will help capture what you think is most important.)

Hollister – a triumph of sign value

At my last visit to the London mega-mall Westfield, there was only one store with a 100-metre queue and a security team at the door. Hollister is a Californian clothing label owned by Abercrombie & Fitch, which describe their style as 'laid-back and effortlessly cool'.[12] What their customers are queuing up for isn't clothing, it's an identity. From the unusually good-looking staff to the music, everything about the Hollister experience is about providing a template of what's cool to a profoundly susceptible demographic. Wearing Hollister makes you one of the cool kids; something of great concern to many teenagers.

Think carefully before adding features

A key take out from this chapter is that not much of our consumer behaviour relates to basic functionality or 'use value'. This is exactly the opposite of how many businesses think, and so they try to increase a product or service's appeal by adding features. This is the kiss of death, especially to technology products: the more features there are the more expensive it gets to add new ones, the more it costs to maintain and, usually, the slower the performance. At the same time it becomes more difficult to use.

There is no better example than the remote control for my television. When people pick it up they just stare at it in horror. The functions you actually want, like turning it on, choosing a channel, changing the volume or controlling the DVD player, are hidden in plain sight among the abundance of useless buttons that nobody ever asked for in the first place. I am not saying that the features and the price point are not important (there are plenty of other books that cover this, so I won't) and, of course, most products find they need a functional minimum to be competitive, but they are just two of the rationales we use; they are not the only ones.

Resolve the tension between individuality and conformity

There is a community dimension to any great brand, and there is an individual one. Since the sign value of a product is often about belonging to a particular group, cultivating a brand community can be especially powerful in reinforcing the sign value. Social media makes this easier than ever. An obvious alternative is to align yourself with an existing community, which is the driving force behind most sponsorship and traditional advertising.

IWC Schaffhausen – a brand community

Swiss watchmaker IWC Schaffhausen has a popular owners' forum on its website. There is an excellent thread on there titled 'Where has your IWC taken you?'[13] where owners upload photos of their watch on their wrist with an interesting scene in the background, like a famous landmark or a beautiful vista. This not only reinforces a sense of global community, but also shows the lifestyles that owners live. It also allows the owner to express their individuality since IWC make a large range of different shapes, sizes and styles.

The other side of the coin is allowing the consumer to express their individuality. This has never been easier with modern technology. Do your customers value conformity and individuality in equal measure? Are they buying in, or expressing their individuality?

Consider your belief structures

Does your brand relate to a particular set of customer beliefs? Think about how these relate to your products and services.

Develop a personality

The inner-directed business has two appealing traits that are often sorely lacking in these modern times: *sincerity* and *personality.* We seem to live in a world where both have been sacrificed on the altar of professionalism. Whenever there is a problem with the trains around where I live, the driver is forced to read the same banal message every time: 'We apologise for any inconvenience this may cause.' When waiting on hold I am often greeted by a monotonous 'your call is very important to us' while I wait endlessly for them to answer. These sterile messages are totally void of any humanity. In a world dominated by shades of grey, adding a bit of colour can go a long way. A bit of personality might just be the difference that keeps your customers coming back.

Air New Zealand – serious fun

In a safety video for Air New Zealand called *Fit to Fly,* a wacky fitness instructor Richard Simmons turns the bland safety procedures into a kind of workout, featuring the captain of the All Black's rugby team among others. Not only does this make a refreshing change, critically it also makes the customer pay more attention to the important message. The video has gone on to become a YouTube hit with over two million views.[17]

Support rationale thinking

The most important conclusion from this chapter is that there is no such thing as rational thinking when it comes to consumer behaviour, only what Rob Walker, author of *Buying In,* cleverly calls *rationale thinking.*[18] Walking down the aisle of the supermarket your inner monologue might go something like this: 'I don't need three of these but they are on special offer (puts in trolley) ... Oh yum cookies! I'm on a diet but these ones are gluten free and I've had a hard day (puts in trolley) ... I need some washing-up liquid ... Oh look this one is more environmentally friendly (puts in trolley).'

We continuously swap between different rationales when we buy and combine them at will, so to come out on top you've got to consider carefully which rationales will apply to your brand and communicate them unambiguously. This is of absolute importance, because it sets the tone for the whole customer experience that follows.

Patagonia

Patagonia are rightly the default example of green-blooded capitalism in action, owing to their absolute commitment to environmental and ethical commitments, but I can't help but feel that this is doing them a slight dis-service: it's not the only rationale for buying their stuff. The reality is they also happen to make products that are extremely well designed, incredibly high quality, and their customer service is excellent. To show they are the real deal, rather than just using good looking models in staged poses, they use photos of real people using their products in real situations in their catalogue. Whatever rationale you want to use, they've got it covered. The founder's book *Let My People Go Surfing* devotes a huge section to their product design philosophy,[19] which I'm sure is central to their success. Few people care if something is eco-friendly if it's also useless: one rationale is rarely enough for anyone.

Build a brand reality, not a brand image

Once you have identified what rationales apply to your business, capture them in a form that can be easily communicated both internally to staff and externally to customers, and then make absolutely sure that they are delivered upon. In my career to date I have sat through countless brand presentations where teams have set out to create a centrally controlled brand image. Most of these miss the point: you need to build a brand reality, not a brand image. Create a great customer experience, and the brand value will look after itself.

John Lewis

How did the department store John Lewis become the darling of the high street? They make true on their commitment to be 'Never knowingly undersold on quality, on price and on service'.[20] Whichever branch you go into, whatever product you are buying, you know you are in safe hands.

Once you have decided on your rationales, you need to commit to them and they need to permeate every single element of the experience. These rationales are the foundation of the customer experience because they set our expectations. We usually become aware of a brand before we do business with them, either through advertising, looking at a website or a referral from a friend. The best way to set yourself up to succeed is to make sure that the initial expectations that are set through marketing or branding can be delivered upon.

Summary

- Wants are a more powerful motivator than needs.

- Social groups define themselves through their consumption.

- Everything we buy reflects our values, beliefs and self-image.

- Great customer experiences help us resolve the tension between expressing our individuality and belonging to a group.

- Think about what your brand says about your customers.

- Focus on creating a brand reality rather than a brand image – this is the foundation of a great customer experience.

5

Great customer experiences satisfy our higher objectives

In a movie, what makes each character interesting are the objectives hidden beneath what they say or do. Customers are no different: wants and needs are derivative, it is satisfying the higher objective behind them that is the foundation on which great experiences are built. This chapter will show you how to model customer objectives in a way that will open up new opportunities for improvements, and help you get your customer experience right at a product or service level.

People don't want to buy a quarter-inch drill, they want a quarter-inch hole! THEODORE LEVITT

The basic purpose of any product or service is to help the customer to satisfy an objective. Customers have goals, and successful products help them to achieve their goals, so before we can make the experience as great as possible, we need to know what this end state looks like. If we are to create a satisfying product or service we must ask ourselves *'What are our customer's goals*?'

Answering this question was relatively straightforward for the pre-Industrial Revolution craftsman. The customer was right there, demanding a table with four legs, made out of wood with a drawer for putting the place-mats in. It is still quite easy for many small businesses which are in close contact with their customers; it's even easier if people are buying something because of who *you* are, like a Damien Hirst artwork.

But what about those businesses which are so large that many employees never have any contact with customers? What about those companies which have more than one distinct type of customer? In my day-to-day work as a design consultant I am often not the intended customer for the product I'm designing. How do I know what these people want? What if you are starting a new business and you aren't really sure who your customer is yet? Now it's not so easy.

Telepathy and empathy

We need to be able to put ourselves in our customer's shoes if we are to understand what their goals are. The best way to do this would be telepathy. In the movie *What Women Want*, advertising exec Nick Marshall (Mel Gibson) has a freak accident that allows him to hear what women are thinking. This leads to all sorts of epiphanies, not least of all that most people dislike his chauvinistic behaviour. He soon realises what a gift this telepathy is: his attitudes to his co-workers, his relationships and his career all improve as he starts to really understand the women around him. As his therapist in the movie says, 'If men are from Mars, and women are from Venus, and you can speak Venutian, the world can be yours.'[1] This neatly summarises one of the primary goals of any business: if we can really understand our customer the world can be ours.

Unfortunately, in the real world we're not telepathic so we must find other ways to understand the customer's goals – we need to build *empathy*. There are several approaches to creating an empathic understanding of the customer. The first is to design something for yourself in the belief that other people will want it too. This approach, known as *self-referential design*, is frowned upon by most user-centered design experts, who insist that it is important to remember that you are not your customer. I don't agree with this.

Designing stuff for people who are like you means you don't need all of the heavy-duty customer and market research because you have an innate feel for what the customer wants. This is how Patagonia got started. It's how 37Signals got started, and it's how Dyson got started. 'Scratching your own itch'[2] is a great way to build a product. 'The quickest way to have empathy for someone else is to be just like them. For companies, the answer is to hire their customers,'[3] writes Dev Patnaik in *Wired to Care*. We often celebrate politicians who are seen as 'a man of the people', we don't tend to praise them as 'a man who was nothing like the people but researched them thoroughly'.

There are, of course, limitations to this. Many businesses succeed because of this initial affinity for their customers, but over time as they get bigger they grow apart, and start hiring people who aren't like their customers. There are also some industries that naturally lend themselves to this more than others. This is where the requirement for research comes from, but this too can be fraught with difficulties.

Shadow dancing

In *The Seven Cs of Consulting* Mick Cope draws a distinction between *surface issues* that we will happily discuss and *shadow issues* which are the hidden thoughts or feelings that we are not comfortable sharing.[4] We might articulate one set of goals but actually have a hidden personal agenda. We may suffer from a phobia that we think is silly, so we let it control our behaviour rather than seek help.

This dissonance between these surface and shadow issues results in that dreaded thing: *office politics.* I've had clients swear blind that they are committed to improving their customer experiences, but actually they aren't at all. They are committed to getting promoted, or sticking to a budget, or getting their contract extended, or making it home for the kids' bath time, or looking good in front of the boss, or paying themselves a bigger dividend this quarter. They may want to make improvements, but that's a surface issue. The shadow issues that are really propelling people's office behaviour go unspoken and unconsidered.

This is not only a problem within the organisation, but also presents itself when conducting customer research. My favourite example comes from Steve Mulder and Ziv Yaar's book *The User is Always Right*: 'When Sony was introducing the boom box, the company gathered a group of potential customers and held a focus group on what colour the new product should be: black or yellow. After some discussion among the group of likely buyers, everyone agreed that consumers would better respond to yellow. After the session, the facilitator thanked the group, and then mentioned that, as a bonus, they were welcome to take a free boom box on the way out. There were two piles of boom boxes: yellow and black. Every person took a black boom box.'[5] Clearly what people say isn't always a true reflection of what they think, so we need a way of getting into these shadowy issues and seeing how they affect the customer's goals.

We can't just ask customers what their goals are, because they probably either can't or won't give a useful answer. We've already explored some of the reasons for this in the previous chapter: during research our *rationale thinking* can get in the way of providing the real insights that the researcher needs. What we need to do is focus on building an empathic connection with the customer rather than just interviewing them, or running workshops or trying to design something collaboratively. Research isn't just something you do at the start of each project. It needs to be about building deeper empathy over time so you are attuned to what they want not just today, but tomorrow. This is rarely how it happens from my experience. The project plan is laid out, and the research is time-boxed at the beginning with some testing and feedback sessions throughout the process. The research usually only consists of swotting over quantitative data with a few focus groups and interviews. This approach will never yield significant improvements.

There is simply no substitute to spending time with your customers. Get to know them, watch them using your stuff, see where they struggle and what they like. Cultivating empathy is more important than collecting analytics and facts. You need to get people out there meeting real customers and experiencing what they experience. The world would be a different place if senior managers spent even a couple of days a year manning the phones on customer services. It would also help if senior managers actually experienced life as a customer. Do you think the CEO of a telecoms company calls the helpdesk if his phone breaks? Do you think the CEO of a car manufacturer gets the same service experience as a typical customer? Of course not, but they should, because without the empathy that comes from these experiences they can't make the right decisions.

Identifying goals

It's clear that the route to identifying our customer's goals is to build an understanding with them, but what exactly do we mean by a goal? Why look at goals and not just the tasks that the customer wants to complete? In Alan Cooper's seminal text on user-centered design, *About Face*, he explains that goals are important because they explain *why* a customer is performing the task in the first place: 'Goals motivate people to perform activities ... Understanding why a user performs certain tasks gives designers great power to improve or even eliminate those tasks, yet still accomplish the same goals.'[6] This is a fundamental part of creating a great customer experience. We need to see how the product or service fits into the bigger picture first, then look at the activities and tasks that the customer must undertake to accomplish their goal. This gives us a basic hierarchy to work within: goals underpin activities, which are in turn composed of tasks. Cooper's work in this area is a useful starting point and I'm going to build on it.

The higher objective

To explain how I think this approach can be improved, I would like to start by using one of Cooper's own examples of a goal. He writes, 'When travelling from St Louis to San Francisco, a person's goals are likely to include travelling quickly, comfortable and safely.'[7] Yes these things are important experiential goals, but he's missing something here: nobody flies to San Francisco just to arrive there, there is a *higher objective* that has caused the flight.

Consider this simple example: Brian and Jenny are on their honeymoon. Steve has a client meeting. James is attending a friend's funeral. They are all flying economy class to San Francisco. Yet for all their similarity, the three have radically different higher objectives, and thinking about them could open up a world of opportunities for the airline.

The honeymooners want a once in a life-time trip, and for them that starts when they leave the house. The business traveller's central requirement is to have a dialogue with his client. Our funeral-goer must get there by any means necessary. Suppose the flight is cancelled or significantly delayed. If you knew the higher objectives of these three distinct customer groups you could: offer the honeymooners entry to the first-class lounge where they can get some unexpected pampering free of charge while they waited; give the business traveller access to a private meeting room where he could have a video conference or at least get some useful work done in a quiet environment; and help the funeral-goer find an alternative route, maybe with another airline or via another airport with a transfer. The opportunities are endless. Just off the top of my head, for the honeymooners you could send them their plane tickets in a congratulations card. This 'reason for travel' information could be captured quite easily during the booking process.

Starting with a simple goal may provide a good experience, but a great one needs to appeal to a higher objective. It is likely that all of your competitors understand the basic goals of their customers as well as you do. It doesn't take a genius to realise that people want to fly comfortably, safely and quickly. To open up opportunities to improve the experience you need to look a little bit further. Forgetting these higher objectives is why so many businesses fail to respond to substitute offerings when they emerge. The recession, terrorism and environmental concerns may all have an impact on air travel, but so does Skype, Instant Messenger and collaborative tools like Basecamp.

The story so far

We have covered a few key points so far in this chapter:

- The kernel of a customer experience is satisfying an objective
- Identifying these objectives comes from having an empathic understanding of the customer
- We all have surface issues and shadow issues, and those shadow issues are often the most powerful drivers of our behaviour

- Looking at goals is more useful than looking at tasks, because they give us a deeper understanding of what customers want
- These goals spring from a higher objective

To bring this all together, what we need is a practical way of building empathy with our customers, understanding their motives, shining a light on their shadow issues and relating all this back to a higher objective. We need to look at our customer experience like an actor looks at a script, always trying to put themselves in the character's shoes. This is exactly what actors do when they use the Stanislavski system.

Mental reconnaissance

Konstantin Stanislavski was a Russian actor born in 1863. He was the first person to create a systematic approach to acting, based on studying what human beings do in their everyday lives. His ideas are incorporated in almost every drama curriculum and their usage is widespread throughout the acting profession. He advocated 'mental reconnaissance',[8] a process of analysing and scrutinising the detail of a script to allow actors to really immerse themselves in their character and hence portray them convincingly.

Stanislavski provides a comprehensive framework for looking beyond what people tell us and what they do, to expose the hidden objectives. He uses five simple concepts that apply equally to a customer experience as they do to a script. These five concepts are explained below and I show you how you can work these into the customer experience.

1 SUPER-OBJECTIVES[9]

A super-objective underpins a whole range of lower objectives. It is our highest level goal. These span a whole range of specific objectives. Start by trying to think about what this might be. The easiest way to do this is to keep asking yourself why a customer would use your product or service until you reach the super-objective. As an example, let's think of a possible super-objective of buying a camera:

The objective is to take a photograph. *Why would we want to do that?*

To capture a moment or scene. *Why would we want to do that?*

So that we can share it.

We now have one possible super-objective: *to share our experiences and the way we see the world with others.*

Kodak have been in business for 133 years and were once the most innovative photographic company in the world, and yet in January this year they filed for bankruptcy protection.[10] Critics have argued that this was because they failed to respond to the digital photography revolution, which may be true, but then again most manufacturers of consumer digital cameras have also suffered as the photographic capabilities of smart-phones have improved. Let's contrast Kodak's fortunes with those which have anchored their business around this super-objective of image sharing: photo sharing platform Instagram has just been sold to Facebook for $1bn,[11] photo-heavy blogging platform Tumblr is now valued at $800 million[12]. A staggering 750 million photos were uploaded to Facebook on New Year's Eve weekend, 2010.[13] People are taking more photos than ever, it's just a shame that Kodak didn't realise why and still don't.

Using either the worksheet from my website (www.mattwatkinson.co.uk/worksheets), or just a piece of paper, start thinking about what your customer's super-objectives might be. There might be more than one of course, but the real purpose of the exercise is to get you to think about your business in a new light and notice new opportunities. Amazon realised that while an objective of their customers might be to order a book, the super-objective was to read the contents, so they created the Kindle reader which did away with the physical book entirely, offering greater convenience and less cost. In the run up to Christmas 2011 they sold over a million Kindles *a week*.[14]

2 SUBTEXT[15]

The subtext is best described as the difference between what people say and what they mean – the underlying thoughts and feelings that are compelling their behaviour. The subtext is the most difficult thing to identify, and yet often is the most powerful driver of customer behaviour.

Look at the information we gathered about the customer's identity in the previous chapter, in particular what rationale they are using, and what sign value may be attached to the product or service. Can you imagine a customer walking into a luxury car dealership and saying to the salesman, 'I'm looking for a status symbol that will make me attractive to the opposite sex. Something that shows to everyone how wealthy and powerful I am'? It's unlikely, but the subtext might be there nevertheless. When playing the lottery the objective is to win, but really in many ways we are paying for the pleasure of *fantasising about winning*. I often wonder how much of giving to charity is more about making ourselves feel good than it is about helping others, although this objective is unlikely to be openly articulated. We need to try our best to identify what the shadowy objective or subtext is. Even just thinking about it for a few minutes can be enough to help us think differently about the customer experience.

3 OBJECTIVES

An objective is the basic reason why somebody performs an activity or task. You need to document these objectives for every stage of the experience, because they form the *success criteria* for the experience. All too often on customer experience projects businesses charge ahead with designing things without having a clear vision of what success looks like. Without this, we don't know whether we've succeeded or failed, we can't test the offering effectively, and the project starts to drift aimlessly because there is no agreed vision for what the team is trying to achieve. Start by identifying objectives that satisfy your super-objective and then gradually break them down.

Returning to our example of the airline, the objective might be to arrive in San Francisco at a certain date and time, but here are some other objectives that feed into that:

- Decide when to go on my trip
- Find the cheapest fare

- Decide how to get to the airport
- Pack appropriately for the length of my stay and the weather at my destination
- Get to the airport on time
- Check in my luggage
- Pass security

Looking at these objectives we can see a world of opportunities. Even if we just consider our objective of packing appropriately, why not e-mail customers a weather forecast for their destination a few days before they go? I invariably forget the international power socket adapter for my laptop so I often have to buy one at the terminal or have to borrow a colleague's at my destination. Why not send an e-mail or SMS with a list of frequently forgotten items to the customer the night before their flight? You could have a YouTube video with tips for how to pack your clothes without getting them crumpled on the flight. I've never received any of these helpful things from an airline, yet they would be relatively inexpensive to do.

To discover these opportunities we need to broaden our definition of the customer experience. I normally start with a blank sheet of paper and working from one objective just keep on writing pre-conditions until I can trace back to the start of the experience, much like I just did with the airline example. I then go the other way and work right down to the end, documenting as many objectives as I can. This is an unstructured and messy task, so don't worry about that. Just start anywhere and follow your nose. You'll quickly find that more and more parts of the experience emerge that you had never considered before.

4 COUNTER-OBJECTIVES[16]

In the real world, we all have different objectives, and a clash is inevitable at some point. This conflict is almost always present between the goals of the customer and the goals of the business: on a simple level, we want a profit and the customer wants value for money – we need to strike a balance here.

More often than not we do not actively consider the relationship between these two conflicting objectives, and there can be dire consequences for both parties. Earlier in the book I told how I have been asked by clients to make their customer service telephone number less visible. This is a classic example of a counter-objective affecting the customer experience. Ignoring these counter-objectives won't make them go away; the best way to resolve the tension between them is to tackle them pro-actively and specifically think of ways to harmonise them.

To do this we need two lists: one of the customer objectives, the other of our business objectives. Start by trying to look for obvious conflicts between the two as in the example above. Identifying the problem is the first step towards solving it. Another approach is to start identifying a list of counter-objectives for each customer objective that has been identified. We also need to consider from the outset what constraints there might be. We never have a limitless budget or timeline and there are often technical constraints about what we can do with the systems we have. Many businesses are strait-jacketed by industry regulations or legal quirks. I have seen businesses waste thousands of pounds because they never considered the constraints upfront.

Here is an example: a customer objective when buying online may be to check out as quickly as possible, yet the business may have a counter-objective of getting customers to set up an account to encourage repeat shopping and allow them to send marketing e-mails. In most e-commerce check-out processes they start by asking if you have an account, in which case you log in, and if not they force you to set one up. Rather than asking them to create an account upfront, a better design is to let them complete the check-out process, entering their address and payment details, then at the end offer them the option to choose a user-name and password to remember their details for future shopping: you have all the other details you need already. It achieves the same result, removes a possible barrier to sales by making the process quicker and is a more customer-centric experience.

We often find that because of technical or legal requirements we have to ask customers to perform an unexpected process, such as completing an additional form, or performing a task in an unusual order. These experiences can be made far more palatable by explaining *why* it needs to be this way. A great example comes from Pret A Manger. On their counter is a sticker that says, 'VAT NIGHTMARE: We're legally required to add on VAT when you eat in.' It's a fun way of explaining why there is a difference between the takeaway and eat in prices of their food and drink, which is in keeping with the personality of the business.

5 STAKES[17]

Every objective has a level of importance to us, which determines how intently we pursue it, and how likely we are to concede to other's counter-objectives. Returning to the airline example again, the stakes are much higher for the funeral-goer than the business traveller.

As customers, when we do not get our way, we are sometimes forced to raise the stakes. It is not uncommon for example, when exasperation sets in, to threaten to take our business elsewhere in order to compel a company to take action. I felt this was necessary when dealing with my mobile phone company recently. I was attempting to re-negotiate my package as I had been misled by them. The customer service agent held firm, until I threatened to leave, at which point I was swapped from the *customer service* department to the *customer retention* department who conceded to my requests. Incidentally this is a great example of how the divisional structures in many large-scale businesses build misleading expectations into the customer experience.

Appreciating what the stakes are reveals another critical aspect of objectives: the more important the objective is, the more becomes invested in it emotionally. Imagine two different bus journeys. In the first I am simply heading into town to go shopping; in the second I am heading to the airport to catch my holiday flight. Consider how I will feel if I am running late and I miss the bus in each different scenario. In the first I may be a little irritated, in the second I might be upset, anxious and angry. I am much more emotional because my objective is more important. Now imagine that the bus driver sees me running to the stop and waits a few seconds for me to get on. In the first situation

I will be thankful for his courtesy, in the second I will be much more grateful.

Bella Merlin, a Stanislavski system expert, describes it this way: 'Emotions arise when something or someone either stops you from achieving or enables you to achieve your objective. The more you need to achieve your objective, the greater will be your emotional response either when you are blocked in your pursuit or when that pursuit is made easier.'[18]

Understanding objectives in the light of their emotional weight is valuable when making improvements to the customer experience. It helps build empathy for the customer and also provides an additional consideration when prioritising which elements to focus on. Satisfying the high-stakes objectives is the route to a great customer experience. Thinking these through in turn is a really useful exercise. Calling your bank to cancel your credit card because you've been mugged is a high-stakes objective. Calling them to change your address has a much lower level of emotional involvement.

Customer profiling #2 – super-objectives and objectives

In the last chapter we saw how Baudrillard's object value system gave us a means of profiling customers on a *brand level* by looking at the sign value, use value and exchange value that appeals to the customer. The categories in Stanislavski's model provide the means of profiling customers on a *product or service level* by looking at the specific objectives that customers have and how they differ. One advantage of looking at the *super-objectives* rather than simply the *objectives* is that there are usually very few distinct differences. It is all too easy to end up with too many profiles, which makes the design process unmanageable. Try to keep the number of profiles to a minimum, only creating a new one where the distinction is clear enough to warrant it.

Summary

- The kernel of a customer experience is satisfying an objective.

- Identifying these objectives comes from having an empathic understanding of the customer.

- We all have surface issues and shadow issues, and those shadow issues are often the most powerful drivers of our behaviour.

- Looking at goals is more useful than looking at tasks, because they give us a deeper understanding of what customers want.

- We can use Stanislavski's system of 'mental reconnaissance' to help us empathise with our customers and identify their objectives.

- The super-objective is the highest level goal for the customer, and the practical objectives spring from it.

- There may be a subtext – a set of unspoken objectives that are really driving the customer's behaviour.

- Objectives often come into conflict with counter-objectives or constraints that must be actively considered from the beginning.

- Every objective has a stake – the higher the stakes are the more emotionally involved we are in achieving that objective. Thinking about the stakes involved can help us prioritise which elements of the experience to focus on.

6

Great customer experiences leave nothing to chance

To create consistent, smooth customer journeys, every interaction needs to be considered, planned and designed. There is no detail that is too small to consider. This chapter will show you how to break the customer experience down into manageable chunks, so that each interaction can be considered and improved.

Good design is thorough down to the last detail. Nothing must be arbitrary or left to chance. Care and accuracy in the design process show respect towards the consumer. DIETER RAMS

There is one simple point to this chapter: *there is no element of the customer experience that is too small to make a difference.* Consider this extract from Robert Greene's *The Art of Seduction.*

> *From the 1940s on into the early 1960s, Pamela Churchill Harriman had a series of affairs with some of the most prominent and wealthy men in the world. What attracted these men, and kept them in thrall, was not her beauty or her lineage or her vivacious personality, but her extra-ordinary attention to detail. It began with her attentive look as she listened to your every word, soaking up your tastes. Once she found her way into your home, she would fill it with your favourite flowers, get your chef to cook that dish you had only tasted in the finest restaurants. You mentioned an artist you liked? A few days later that artist would be attending one of your parties. She found the perfect antiques for you, dressed in the way that most pleased or excited you, and she did this without saying a word … Harriman's attention to detail had an intoxicating effect on all the men in her life.*

Life is harsh and competitive. Attending to detail in a way that is soothing to the other person makes them dependent upon you ... Anyone can say the right words ... the gesture, the thoughtful gift, the little details seem much more real and substantial.[1]

Attention to detail is not only the secret to seduction, it is also one of the secrets to a great customer experience. We care about details, because they show that the business cares about us.

The aggregation of marginal gains

There is another reason why details matter: the total customer experience is really just the sum of the smaller interactions. If you improve everything you do, even just by a little bit, these tiny gains add up to something big, an approach the legendary GB cycling coach David Brailsford calls 'the aggregation of marginal gains'.[2]

In my experience, clients who want to improve their customer experience start by kicking off a project, and the higher their aspirations the bigger this project gets: more stakeholders, bigger changes, timelines and budgets. It starts with a grand, strategic vision and ends in tears. To start with it takes too long to agree on the scope of the project, then when it moves into a feasibility assessment they realise the whole technical infrastructure of the company needs to be replaced which doubles the workload and creates more dependencies. Requirement documents swell from a few pages to a few hundred pages. In short, it becomes an unmanageable mess. Nothing gets delivered, or if it does it's usually so late as to be irrelevant, or so expensive as to offer no return. Have you ever looked at a company's products or website and thought to yourself *'Why don't they just fix it?'* This is most likely the reason why they haven't. They aren't trying to fix small problems. They are trying to change the entire universe and failing.

One alternative is to look for 'quick wins', which is a more pragmatic approach, but most often 'quick win' really means 'slow fail'. In practice it is usually something that can be bodged easily, rather than a small issue we can do a thorough job on. Quick wins make things far worse later on, and often don't really make things better in the short term.

Clients most often succeed by delivering smaller projects. Little and often works best. You want the lowest number of the best possible people, working to a clear and achievable objective. If they are smart they can manage themselves. If they are committed you don't need to keep an eye on them: just give them the brief and let them get on with it. Most projects would be more successful with a smaller scope, shorter timelines, smaller budgets and fewer people.

Stages and steps

In Chapter 4 we discovered how great customer experiences reflect the customer's identity. This helps us improve the experience at a *brand level*. In Chapter 5 we saw that great customer experiences satisfy our higher objectives. This helps to get the experience right at a *product or service level*. This chapter completes the hierarchy by looking at the customer experience at an *interaction level*, which gives us a complete structure to work within when trying to identify areas to improve.

You can't infuse the experience with the right brand values if you don't know what they are upfront, and you can't evaluate whether features or functions are useful without relating them back to the customer's higher objectives. But both these things – the brand promise and the higher objectives – are delivered through each and every interaction the customer has with the business. To create a great customer experience we need to identify what these interactions are.

The temptation is always to charge in and start designing stuff or bouncing exciting ideas around, because this is the most fun part, but before we get into that we need to know exactly what needs to be designed. I find it easiest to do this by breaking the customer journey down into two levels that I call *stages* and *steps*. I do this for four reasons:

1 Distinguishing between broad stages made up of small steps allows us to look at the experience at different levels of detail. It's useful to have a bigger picture to refer back to because it's easy to get lost in the minutiae when you get into the small interactions.

2 Breaking the experience down into a sequence of small steps allows us to understand all the dependencies between different stages before it's too late. There's nothing worse on a project than having to re-design whole chunks because you missed a key dependency.

3 Looking at the customer experience as a series of small steps allows us to get the sequence of events in the correct order so the experience flows seamlessly from end to end.

4 It helps us identify and prioritise the problems within the experience, so we can concentrate our efforts in a way that gives real-world improvements quickly. It can also help us to keep projects to a manageable size.

Identifying stages

At this point in the process we know what the experience must be like on a brand level, and we have used Stanislavski's *mental reconnaissance* techniques to identify the customer's objectives. Starting with the *super-objectives* and *objectives* of the most important customer profile, start writing down the stages of the customer experience that are required to satisfy them.

The question you are trying to answer is 'What does the customer need to do to satisfy their objectives?' Referring back to our airport example, the question becomes 'What does James *need to do* to get to the funeral in San Francisco on time?'

A mental re-run of my last flight gives me the following stages as a starting point:

- **Plan the trip**
- **Find the best fare**

- **Buy a ticket**
- Pack
- Get to the airport
- **Check in**
- Clear security
- **Wait in departures**
- Go to the gate
- **Board the plane**
- **Fly to destination**
- **Disembark**
- Pass immigration
- Collect luggage
- Meet friends at arrivals
- Leave airport
- Arrive at destination

We can see even from this example that there can be far more parts to the experience than we consider. My experience of air travel is that investment in the customer experience is limited to those stages in **bold** – fewer than half of them!

There are two approaches you can try to get started with identifying stages if you aren't sure what they might be. One way is to think of the customer's journey on the highest level first then work down. For example, you might start with four simple stages that apply to most businesses:

1 Discovering the brand
2 Shopping
3 Using the product or service (commonly called 'in-life service')
4 After-sales support

You could then break these down into smaller stages. If we were evaluating the experience for a supermarket we might take the stage *shopping* and split it down further. By the way, it's always useful to give stages and steps a unique reference number in case you end up sharing them with colleagues.

SHOPPING STAGES

2.1 Orientating yourself in the shop

2.2 Browsing the products available

2.3 Asking staff for help with finding a product

2.4 Taking products to the check-out

2.5 Checking out

2.6 Taking the products to the car

Scenarios are helpful

A popular technique to help identify the stages of a customer journey is to write out a quick scenario to help guide your thinking, using the different profiles from the previous chapter as a starting point.

An example might be, 'Mrs Miggins is doing her weekly food shop, as she does every Saturday morning.' Or, 'Clive is popping in to the supermarket on his way home from a long day at work to get something quick and easy for dinner that evening.' You can do as many scenarios as you like, and add as little or as much detail as you like to help get your brain going. Scenarios are like scaffolding – they are there to help you, but they aren't what you are designing. Don't worry about formally covering every possible eventuality. This will all come out in the wash as you get into more detail.

Define the success criteria

It is essential to give each stage a set of success criteria to judge it by. This should be straightforward to do, since you can use the objectives you identified in the previous chapter as a starting point. I would include the business objectives for each stage in the success criteria too, so you can start to identify any conflicts between the two that may need to be resolved. The remaining chapters of the book will give you much more to work with when defining these criteria, but for now it is enough to note down what the customer's objectives are so that they remain in the front of your mind at all times.

Success criteria not only help to keep the experience on track, but they also help to build consensus within the project team about what you are really trying to achieve. If you can't relate a stage directly back to clearly defined objectives you need to think these through before you go any further. Success criteria are also vital for testing – if we don't know what success looks like, we won't know if we've succeeded. Here are some possible success criteria for the stage 'Taking the products to the car'.

TAKING THE PRODUCTS TO THE CAR – CUSTOMER SUCCESS CRITERIA

- I can find my way out of the store easily
- I can find my car easily in the car-park
- I can move my goods to the car without damaging them
- I can load my shopping into the car without difficulty
- I can leave my trolley somewhere convenient for me

TAKING THE PRODUCTS TO THE CAR – BUSINESS OBJECTIVES

- Upsell more goods on the way out – coffee, newspapers, magazines, petrol
- Minimise theft or damage to property – trolleys, etc.
- Restrict car-park usage to our customers only

Even at this seemingly unimportant stage we can expose issues. Here are a few from my own experience:

- My local supermarket is in the middle of a town, and operates their car-park on a 'pay and display' basis to try to restrict its usage to customers. Although they refund the price of the parking at the check-out it is annoying to have to keep loose change with you whenever you want to go there. Some shoppers find they return to their car to a parking fine because they weren't aware it was a paying car-park. This is especially bad if you have just paid the business in question for your food shopping.

- In an attempt to reduce trolley theft and incentivise customers from leaving them randomly around the car-park some shops force you to put a pound coin into the trolley to release it. This is extremely annoying.

- One supermarket near me uses giant revolving doors on the exit. This is terrible to try and navigate with a trolley, especially for families who also have a push-chair.

- It is also common to have to walk a long way to the trolley-park because the shop is more interested in maximising the number of parking spaces. The result is that trolleys just get left anywhere which can do damage to customers' cars and requires someone from the shop to find and collect them.

- I've had bags split when carrying them to the car because they were too flimsy and were torn by the corner of some packaging.

- Walking a long way to the car can mean you and your shopping get soaked if it starts to rain.

- Elderly shoppers or those with small children may struggle to get their goods to the car, either because they are too heavy or they have too many other things to carry.

Each of these issues is an opportunity in disguise. Here are a few things we could consider, though I'm sure there are many more opportunities than I've covered:

- Customers could pay for parking using their loyalty card if they have one.

- The shop could provide tokens at the reception desk in case a customer doesn't have change.

- Staff could be on duty at the doors with umbrellas to walk the customer to their car when it was raining. This wouldn't have to cost anything – staff who were normally collecting trolleys could do it.

- Staff could be on hand to help take customers' shopping to their cars. This might be further improved by asking the customer if they would like this service when they arrive at the check-out rather than afterwards to avoid any waiting around. If they were asked when they arrived at the supermarket it might encourage them to buy more if they knew they did not have to worry about carrying it back to the car.
- A large sign at the entrance of the car-park and the supermarket reminding you to bring your own bags from the car would help minimise the use of plastic bags. We often have bags, we just forget to bring them from the car.

Start at the start and end at the end

When looking at the stages of the customer experience, try to trace the experience all the way back to the beginning then right to the end. We touched on this earlier when looking at the stages involved in air travel. It's always been my experience that businesses focus on too narrow an area and so miss opportunities.

Sticking with the supermarket theme, an excellent example of the value of broadening your horizons is online grocery shopping. Supermarkets focus on making items easy to find on the website, remembering items you shopped for previously and providing a good delivery service, but the experience actually starts way before the customer visits the website, and it ends way after the goods have been delivered. What triggers a supermarket shop? You could open the cupboard to find you've run out of something; you could be cooking a meal for friends at the weekend; you could have a regular routine that you go to the same supermarket every Saturday morning and buy broadly the same things every time; you could want to try something new to eat, or even be starting a new diet. Either way, whenever you buy food there is some sort of planning involved, especially if you are going to do the shop online.

This planning stage is woefully neglected. Often, to find a recipe you might want to try, you need to know upfront what that recipe is – they don't make helpful suggestions for things to try – and integration with the rest of the shopping experience is weak. If they know you are ordering all the ingredients for a recipe from the website, why don't they include a print out of it with the shopping when it arrives? Some online retailers do not even allow you to add the ingredients for a recipe straight to the basket.

If I know I am at home for breakfast five days this week, for dinner three days, and want to take a healthy lunch to work for four, why can't a website present me with options for doing exactly that rather than making me trawl through all the products myself? Why not have an option to start the shop with a calendar view rather than a search box? All they are doing is trying to transpose the in-store experience onto a new medium, rather than taking advantage of the technology available on the web.

Supercook.com – perfect planning

This website allows you to enter ingredients that you already have, then it recommends meals that you can make either using only those ingredients or by adding a few more. It makes the whole process of discovering recipes easier by cleverly prompting you for other ingredients that you may have, and also allows you to input ingredients that you want to exclude from the recommendations. This is a totally different approach from the usual one of endlessly browsing recipes based on cuisine, or keyword searches.

Break the stages down into steps

Once you have all the stages, you can break them down into the specific steps that are involved. For the stage *checking out* at a supermarket this may consist of:

STEPS WITHIN THE STAGE – CHECKING OUT

1 Find the check-out with the shortest queue
2 Load the items from the basket onto the check-out stand

3 Scan the items

4 Pack them into bags

5 Pay for the items

They may seem small, but each step is an opportunity to make improvements. The best thing about the steps and stages approach is that you can keep breaking both of them down as the project progresses. You can start big and then keep zooming in until no stone is unturned. You will never discover every step straight away, and it's a messy, time-consuming process, but it's worth doing and re-doing. Don't be too concerned with working in a linear way. I often find it helps to just start anywhere then work outwards.

Waitrose – check-out process

Of the UK supermarkets Waitrose has the best check-out experience by far. At my local store staff are always smartly dressed, always smile and they ask how you are when you get to the till. They treat the items with care as they scan them, and as a nice touch they always open any egg carton to check that none of the eggs has been broken. If you have forgotten an item they will happily call someone to scurry off and get it for you. As a final flourish, you are given a green token at the end to put into one of three charity boxes on the way out, which decides how Waitrose will divide up the £1000 a month that they donate to local charities.

Let's contrast this with Tesco, which at the time of writing have just issued their first profit warning in two decades. Comments from customers on *The Guardian*'s Reality Check are revealing: 'The first thing you are asked at the check-out is for your loyalty card, rather than a simple (but appreciated) hello.'[3] Another customer comments that 'They've lost the human touch. You get poor service … You don't have much personal contact. Tesco has taken people off the shop floor. You go into the Co-op or Waitrose and you get charming, well-informed staff. In Tesco you have to search for them … Actually it's the consumer that's doing all the work.'[4]

Instead of trying to improve the check-out experience for the customer, Tesco have opted to try and automate it by implementing

▶

more self-check-outs. Referring back to the first chapters of this text, this is classic, rational, measurebating in action – self-check-outs mean fewer staff, which means fewer costs. The reality is that it isn't actually improving things at all. Writing in *The Sunday Times*, Daisy Goodwin hits the nail on the head when she says, 'If you want an anonymous, impersonal retail experience, you can shop online ... Self-service is a scam – cost-cutting masquerading as customer convenience ... most of us are more likely to be loyal to the shop where there is a helpful member of staff who is more than happy to find the low-fat yoghurts or who smiles at us at the end of a long, hard week ... Personal service isn't a thing of the past – it's the successful business strategy of the future.'[5] Tesco seem to agree at last, with CEO Philip Clarke admitting they have taken 'a little bit too much away from the shopper' and are committing £1 billion to making over their UK stores, and hiring 8000 new staff.[6]

User profiling #3 – significant factors

When we look at the smallest steps involved in a customer journey, we find that the number of things that affect a customer's decision making can grow. Consider our supermarket – these might include: whether the customer has a loyalty card, whether they are paying by cash or credit or debit card, whether they are using a basket or a trolley. Each of these is a *significant factor* in the design of the customer journey. A customer who is using a wheelchair may need help getting items from high shelves or might need a specially designed trolley, and yet these factors will not usually be picked up at the higher levels of profiling – the identity or objective level – even though they are very important. What we need to do is generate a complete list of significant factors that apply to the stage, then group them into combinations.

Start by generating the largest list possible of factors – *Are they an existing customer or a new customer? Have they registered for an online service or not? Is the customer logged in or not? Are they doing these steps online or in a shop? Are they in a particular location – at home, in the office, on a train platform?* This list of possible factors can grow very quickly, and you may find even more emerge as you read the rest of the chapters. Factors such as competence – *is the customer a beginner, intermediate or expert?* – can be of huge importance when designing an interaction. The point is to keep adding to the list and accept that you won't know everything at the start. I worked with a client recently who charged ahead and designed a service only to find it alienated a large percentage of their customers because they missed a factor – don't repeat their mistake.

Once you have the list of significant factors, the key is to prioritise them by looking at the most important combinations of factors. Suppose we identify three significant factors for the *registration* stage of an online supermarket: whether they have a loyalty card, whether they live in the delivery area, and how they are registering. These variables result in the possible combinations shown in Figure 6.1.

For example:

- Combination 1 – *has loyalty card, lives within delivery area, is registering online* – is an obvious one to work on since it allows the best experience for the customer. We might be able to

Figure 6.1 Possible combinations of significant factors for the registration stage of an online supermarket

		Combinations							
		1	2	3	4	5	6	7	8
Significant factors	**Has loyalty card**								
	Yes	●		●		●		●	
	No		●		●		●		●
	Lives within delivery area								
	Yes	●	●			●	●		
	No			●	●			●	●
	Registration method								
	Online	●	●	●	●				
	In-store					●	●	●	●

pre-populate a large number of the registration form fields for the customer by using the data attached to their loyalty card, which saves them time. If we know their address we might be able to auto-check whether we can deliver to them, to save them having to go through this process manually too.

- Combination 4 – *no loyalty card, lives outside the delivery area, is registering online* – is another good one to work on, since it represents the worst-case scenario. The customer must enter all the information manually, only to find out that we do not deliver to them. Combinations 2 and 3 re-use elements from 1 and 4, so we don't need to worry about them so much because they are not unique.

For the stage you are working on, start with one or two combinations, and then document the steps required to meet the objectives successfully.

Specifically enter waiting times

If there is a significant wait time between one step of a journey and the next, add it to the list as its own step. If you know about these wait times there is a chance you can minimise them. If you don't note them down, they won't be improved.

Look at the sequencing and dependencies

Every customer journey has some dependencies between steps. If they are not actively addressed, they impact negatively on the experience. When I first started looking into online grocery shopping for a project I was working on, I found that some retailers would allow me to get all the way to checking out with a full basket of goods, to then tell me that they didn't deliver to my area. Some took the opposite approach, forcing me to create an account before I could even have a look at what was available. Neither are great solutions.

If you are working on one specific stage of the experience, it is critical to model all the dependencies that come before that stage. If you don't, you run the risk of designing something that doesn't work, or having a scope that creeps further and further up-stream to incorporate the dependencies into the project.

To move the dependencies out into the open so that they can be addressed, whenever you discover one add it to a list of *pre-conditions* for each stage. In the example above, the dependency is that the supermarket can deliver to the address, so a pre-condition for the stage *shopping* is that the address can be delivered to. A far better solution for the supermarkets would be to have a call out box on the homepage that says something like, 'First time shopping here? Enter your post code to check we deliver to you first.' Of course, not every step of every customer experience is performed in the same sequence every time, but where there are sequential processes they need to be considered end-to-end.

Map out all the touchpoints

One of the biggest challenges for creating a great customer experience can be joining up all the touchpoints. We might use the website, a mobile app, a kiosk, a shop, or phone a call centre on our customer journey. There may be more than one touchpoint we can use to complete a given task. To address this problem, for every step you note down, you also need to write down what touchpoint the customer is using, or which ones it may be useful for them to use. I recommend documenting your *as is* customer experience, as well as your *to be* one. Your *as is* model will expose all of the broken joints and inconsistencies between different touchpoints which you can improve in the future.

I produce two diagrams to help with this. The first is a simple grid with the touchpoints on one axis, e.g. shop, call centre, e-mail, social media, website, mobile app, then the stages of the experience along the other axis, e.g. browse products, add product to basket, check out, specify delivery time. Then within each square note down what offerings there are, e.g. does our mobile app allow us to check out? Could we use social media to raise awareness of new products? Often the simple act of mapping these two variables together generates all sorts of new ideas that you had not considered. It also brings to the surface any obvious disconnects between the different touchpoints you have. See Figure 6.2 below for an example.

The second diagram that I find useful is a swimlane diagram that shows how the customer moves between touchpoints along their journey. You start by drawing a series of parallel horizontal lines, each of which represents a touchpoint. Then, giving each step of the journey a number, you add them onto the swimlanes in sequence. It will end up looking like a line graph, which shows how the customer moves between the different touchpoints along their journey. See Figures 6.3 and 6.4 for an example.

This kind of diagram is useful because it helps other members of the team to understand how the journey really looks. It also further helps to expose dependencies. When you start to look at allowing customers to perform tasks on various touchpoints the dependencies get much more complex.

Figure 6.2 The possible touchpoints I can use for the different stages of my train journey to London

Location	Stage	Touchpoint						
		Website	Mobile app	Telephone system	Parking meter	Ticket kiosk	Departure screen	Ticket office
At home	1 Check train times for next morning	●	●					
	2 Check live departure times for any delays	●	●					
Car-park	3 Car-park							
	4 Pay for parking ticket			●	●			
Rail station	5 Buy rail ticket					●		
	6 Check departure platform	●	●				●	●

To show these two kinds of diagram in action, I have mapped the first part of my train journey to London in Figure 6.2, which shows some of the stages I complete when I travel to London on the train and the possible touchpoints I can use. Here you can see that to pay for my parking at the car-park, I must use a telephone system where I enter my vehicle registration and credit card details, or pay with cash at a kiosk in the car-park. I then go on to use another kiosk or the ticket office to buy my train ticket, and can then use another screen to check which platform my train departs from.

The swimlane diagram in Figure 6.3 shows my typical journey in the morning and what touchpoints each interaction uses. I start by checking the train times the night before, using the mobile app. Before I leave the house I use the app again to see if there are any delays on the line. I then drive to the station, park in the car-park and pay for my ticket using their telephone parking system. I then use the kiosk at the station to buy my ticket, then check the departure screen for which platform I need.

Looking at this I can see two improvements straight away. First of all, I am using two separate touchpoints both of which require a credit/ debit card transaction for two different tasks: paying for parking,

Figure 6.3 A swimlane diagram of the different touchpoints I use during different stages at the start of my journey to London

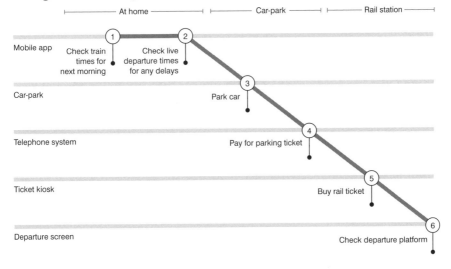

and buying my rail ticket. The first improvement I would make here would be to allow the customer to pay for parking when buying the rail ticket using the ticket kiosk. This would reduce the number of transactions the customer needs to complete, and make them less likely to forget to pay for parking using the phone system if they are in a rush. The second improvement I would make is that while the customer is waiting for the ticket to print at the kiosk, it could show on the screen the next trains that matched the ticket they had bought and what platform they were on. This would further simplify the customer journey, saving the customer time and effort. The resulting customer journey is shown below in Figure 6.4.

Figure 6.4 My journey to London after some minor re-modelling

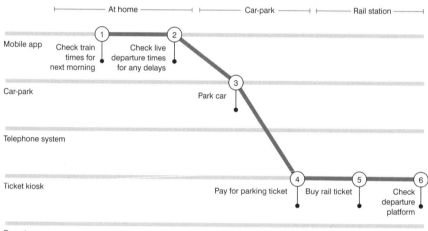

Identity, objectives, stages and steps

The first three chapters of this text should have helped you to create a complete two-dimensional breakdown of the customer experience: looking at the experience from top to bottom we should now know how the brand experience must relate to the customer's identity first and foremost, how the product or service experience must relate to their super-objectives, and on an interaction level, what tasks the customer must undertake as part of the experience, broken down first into stages, then into steps.

Looking at the experience chronologically, we now also know where the experience really begins and where it ends. This may be cyclical or linear, but we should now know every event, and the sequence in which they take place. Now we've got the flesh and bones of the experience, the rest of the book shows you how to bring it all to life by making each of these interactions as good as it can be. Before we move on though, here are four beautiful sets of details to inspire you.

Vitsoe – beautiful shelving

It is no surprise that the attention to detail of Vitsoe shelving is extraordinary, since the system was designed by Dieter Rams, the author of the quotation at the start of this chapter. Each shelving system comes with a free spirit level the exact width of the shelf to make hanging them as easy as possible. Each of the different types of screws comes in its own reusable canvas bag. The packaging folds flat and can be re-used if you move house and want to take your shelves with you, which of course you would, such is the quality of their design and construction. These are just a few of the great details of their system. The details constantly reinforce the company's values too – minimal waste, re-use, longevity and, of course, excellence in design. If a company can make hanging shelves an amazing experience, then you have no excuse!

Leica – the perfect un-boxing experience

The packaging of Leica cameras is designed to make un-boxing one for the first time a beautiful experience in itself. Again, this is a great detail that also reinforces the key brand values – quality and precision. Type 'Leica Unboxing' into YouTube to see for yourself.

Dyson – sits on stairs

Thinking through the specific steps of completing a task can reveal great opportunities to innovate. My small Dyson vacuum cleaner is cleverly designed to allow it to sit on the stairs, which makes it much easier to use. Without explicitly considering how people vacuum-clean their houses it would be easy to miss this detail. So easy in fact that before Dyson I'm not aware of a cleaner that has this design feature. In fact, you could argue that the entire bagless Dyson system came from evaluating one step – emptying the dirt from the vacuum cleaner. There could be a billion dollar idea lurking in one small step of your customer experience.

Viking Stationery

When my stationery order arrived from Viking, the paper invoice that I am used to finding scrunched up at the bottom of the packaging was within a re-usable plastic wallet, that I now use for keeping my writing drafts in. Will I order stationery anywhere else? Unlikely.

Summary

- We care about details because they show that the business cares about us.

- If every detail is right, the overall experience will be right – lots of small gains create one large gain.

- Breaking the experience down into steps and stages reveals the details.

- Every stage of the experience needs to have documented success criteria.

- Tracing the experience right back to the start, then right down to the end reveals opportunities to innovate.

- Identifying the dependencies between stages as early as possible reduces risk on the project.

- Breaking the big stages down into small steps reveals opportunities for improvements.

- The steps that a customer takes depends on the combination of significant factors that applies to them.

- Modelling how customers move between touchpoints is the key to creating seamless multi-channel experiences.

7

Great customer experiences set and then meet expectations

Existing expectations, learnt behaviours and associations are the criteria that customers use to judge an experience from the beginning. Great customer experiences explicitly consider these factors, and exceed expectations where desirable. This chapter shows you how and when to set, meet and exceed expectations along the whole customer journey to make your experience the best it can be.

Happiness equals reality minus expectations. TOM MAGLIOZZI

A few years ago I went to a dealership to buy my dream car. I'd been constructing the fantasy since childhood, and I could see in my mind's eye exactly how it was going to be: the fawning salesman and gleaming bodywork, the first turn of the key. The reality, of course, never lived up to the dream. I never envisaged waiting around or signing endless bits of paper. They didn't slowly lift a silk cover revealing my pride and joy either – it was in the car-park when I arrived to collect it. Worst of all, I didn't feel special like I thought I would.

The wonderful quote, 'Expectation is the root of all heartache' is true indeed – nothing ruins a customer experience like unmet expectations. Parcels that don't turn up on time, products that look nothing like the brochure, the dreaded small print. The more excited we are, the more disappointing the shortfall is.

To put the scale of the problem (or opportunity) into context, according to a 2008 study by Accenture, a massive 68 per cent of electronic goods returned to shops are not actually broken, they simply didn't meet expectations.[1] Reporting on the study for the Inquirer, Nick Farrell puts it concisely: 'Retailers and vendors could save a fortune if they spent more time producing instructions that were easy to understand and marketing material that did not promise the moon on a spoon.'[2]

The only measure of an experience that really matters is how the real world compares to the dress rehearsal in your head. The rest of the principles in this book count for nothing if the experience doesn't meet expectations. You can have a better experience staying at a $100 motel than a $4000 suite. You can have a better flight on a budget carrier than travelling first class. It's all down to expectations.

The science of expectation

Expectations are so critical because they are fundamental to how the brain works. The dopamine neurons in our brain that are responsible for regulating our emotions work by generating patterns based on experience: they trigger emotions based on predictions.

When everything goes according to our predictions these dopamine neurons fire up and we experience pleasurable positive emotions. However, if our expectations turn out to be wrong, the neurons stop firing and we feel upset. The brain is designed to accentuate the impact of these mistakes. As soon as an outcome does not match an expectation the brain sits up and pays attention: few things generate such a powerful emotional response as surprise because we need to learn from our mistakes in order to survive. This makes unexpected pleasures far more powerful too.

Memory and experience

Nobel Prize winning psychologist Daniel Kahneman makes an interesting observation about the critical role of memory in the context of experience, drawing a distinction between the *experiencing self*, concerned with what is happening in the present, and the *remembering self* who reviews an experience retrospectively.[3] He concludes that 'Memories are all we get to keep from our experience of living, and the only perspective that we can adopt as we think about our lives is therefore that of the remembering self.'[4]

Since our memories of past experiences are used to set expectations for the future, the memories we have of a customer experience are crucial, not just because we want customers to have positive memories, but because it affects the likelihood of repeat business.

Learnt behaviours and associations

Through repetition, we find we are able to do things without consciously thinking about them. Examples of this *automaticity* are abundant: we can walk and talk without tripping over our feet or type without thinking about the keys. We often get home from a long journey to realise we have been driving for a long time, changing lanes, accelerating, braking and checking our mirrors without consciously doing any of it.

These kinds of learnt behaviours only work in conditions that match our expectations: I can type without thinking on a variety of devices only if they all have a QWERTY keyboard. I expect the order of the pedals in a car to be clutch, brake, accelerator. We've all had situations where we try to change our behaviour but do things on auto-pilot, like making a cup of tea for a friend but putting sugar in because that's how we have it. These errors are known as *strong habit intrusions*.[5]

We also develop *associations* over time – smells awaken long forgotten memories and colours take on symbolic meanings; associations which can also apply to brands. People often describe superlative examples in a given market as 'The Rolls-Royce'. Fiat CEO Sergio Marchionne said in an interview, 'I want Fiat to become the Apple of automobiles. And the 500 will be our iPod.'[6]

There are very few experiences that don't involve learnt behaviours and associations in some way. Actively considering them makes sure we are using them to our advantage. We can even make the mundane or tedious more enjoyable by transferring learnt behaviours and associations from more positive experiences.

Expectations – a golden opportunity

Precisely because expectations are so powerful *and* often so poorly handled, expectation management is a golden opportunity. This is great news for you: while your competitors are busy disappointing their customers by not calling them back, breaking promises and over-hyping their new offerings, you can be building a reputation for reliability and trustworthiness. I have often thought that all a courier would need to do to sew up the market is deliver when they say they will and pro-actively let you know if they are running late, or can't find your address. Nobody has managed this yet from my experience!

To make expectation management work in your favour all we need to look at is *how* and *when* expectations get *set* and *met* throughout the experience; how we can leave customers with the most positive memories of their experiences; and also consider any existing *learnt behaviours* and *associations* that may come into play. The rest of this chapter shows you how to do this in practice.

Expectation mapping

Part of the reason that companies struggle to manage expectations is because of the divisional structures often found in organisations. As we move along our customer journey, each stage is often presided over by a different department with different motives, so it's no wonder we often end up with conflicting expectations. The advertising team want to create desire for the product, sales teams are often on commission. Neither of them actually design the product itself. Customer services teams often pick up the pieces at the end.

This is why we often find ourselves seduced by a fantastic advert only for the product to disappoint, or enjoy a fantastic product only to find the customer service is terrible – different teams, different motives. It seems crazy when you think about it, but most businesses do not pro-actively manage customer expectations, even though they know they are important. I've yet to work in an organisation where explicit consideration of expectations across the customer journey is part of the design process. Let's put this right!

Expectations cascade from the top down. What we expect from the brand applies to the product or service, then to every little interaction. To provide a great experience, we need to see the customer experience as one long journey, and a continuous process of *setting* and *meeting* expectations. Since we have already broken the customer journey down into broad stages containing smaller steps, all we need to do is model what the customers' expectations are *at the beginning of each stage or step*, and what *subsequent expectations are set by it*. By doing this we can not only expose any risks of misaligned expectations, but we can ensure that the customer knows what to expect from the very start of their experience to the very end.

To do this you just need a sheet of paper or a spreadsheet with three columns (or the worksheet available on my website at www.mattwatkinson.co.uk/worksheets). In the first column you put the stage or step name (depending on the level of detail you are looking at), in the second column you put 'existing expectations', then in the third column you put 'set expectations'.

- *Existing expectations* are those that the customer has already when they commence this stage of the experience, for example when they arrive at an airline's website, they expect to be able to search for flights.
- *Set expectations* are those that arise as the result of an interaction, for example once they have checked in online, they expect that they will not have to queue to check in at the airport terminal.

Once you have this list you can get to work on identifying issues. These are typically caused by three things:

1 *Dissonance* – the set expectation not matching the reality
2 *Absence* – expectations not being set at all
3 *Inference* – the customer's expectations being set elsewhere

MINIMISING DISSONANCE

A classic example of dissonance comes from a company I met which told me a major cause of customer disappointment was when they had to send an engineer out to repair one of their products. Their advertising said that their response time was four hours on average, however this was only the average. It could be up to eight hours. Customers who saw the advert focused on the 'four hours' and so anything longer was a disappointment.

Dissonance is the most common form of expectation failure: saying one thing, then doing something else. This is why it is important to consider both *set* and *met* expectations so you can look for differences between them. Once you identify a gap you can then decide whether to set a different expectation or adjust the real-world experience to meet it. If you say you are going to do something, you *must do it*. This alone will stand you above the competition in most cases.

ABSENCE – FILLING THE VOID

Failing to set expectations at all can be a major source of frustration. None of us likes to be kept in the dark. Ask yourself *'What expectations are going unmanaged?'*

INFERENCE – DON'T LEAVE EXPECTATIONS TO THE IMAGINATION

I recently worked with a private health company which had big problems with expectation management, caused by *inference*. Customers assumed that when they had private health cover they could just go and book treatments with consultants or practitioners only to find that they weren't covered because they hadn't used an approved facility or professional, or that the treatment wasn't covered in their policy. They also assumed that because they now had private cover they no longer needed to use the National Health Service for anything, which isn't correct either. This has dire consequences for both the business and the customer: the business is unfairly branded as reluctant to pay out, and the customer is left with an unexpected bill that could run into thousands.

The policy literature states that there is a process that must be followed to get private treatment, but customers do not always read the details and therefore make incorrect assumptions. The solution was to communicate the process more clearly, providing a simple step-by-step set of instructions that explained: what to do, what you should have done already, and what happens next for each step of the process, to make sure that accurate expectations were set at all times.

Often what a customer expects isn't set by the business at all. It can come from a friend recommending something, a reputation in the market, or even from competitors. If everybody else offers online check-in and we don't, even if it's for a great reason, we need to manage that expectation upfront, rather than leaving the customer to ferret around on the website looking for a feature that doesn't exist. Ask yourself *'What expectations are being set that are out of our control, and how can we address them? What assumptions is the customer making about our product or service and are they accurate?'*

Here are some general rules that can help you further improve your expectation management.

Aim for consistency

Consistent behaviour leads to accurate expectations, and is the bedrock on which trust is built. We want to know what is stable today to establish what we think will happen in the future. There can be little trust without reliability. Aim to create a consistent experience not just across customers, but along the duration of the experience, so each stage is of an equal standard. This not only helps with expectation management, it reinforces what the brand stands for when the values are demonstrated with absolute consistency. If our experiences are of a consistently high standard it also makes the odd blip more forgivable! Ask yourself *'How can we make the experience of a consistent standard for each customer, and at every stage of the journey?'* Again, this is where knowing each step of the experience from start to finish will be invaluable to identify the wrinkles that need smoothing out.

Design a future memory

Daniel Kahneman, whose work on memory and experience we looked at earlier in the chapter, also conducted pioneering research on a phenomenon know as *the peak-end rule*, which shows that our memory of an event is most influenced by the severity of pain at its greatest magnitude – the peak – and by how well or badly the experience ends.[7]

We can put the peak-end rule to good use: thinking about the peaks in the experience and how each interaction ends makes an excellent means to prioritise areas for improvement: minimising any negative spikes first, and making sure the end of each interaction is the best it can be. Returning to our air travel example, since we usually have to surrender any fluids beforehand, why not have staff on the other side of the security point giving out free bottles of water? This would certainly give us a better memory of what is quite a negative, invasive experience.

Make somebody responsible for the customer experience

The customer experience requires ownership and leadership in the same way that a building needs an architect or a movie needs a director. Somebody needs to have overall responsibility and accountability for the customer experience who is not blinkered by the typical departmental boundaries, especially if the customer experience involves multiple touchpoints.

This person – let's call them the Chief Experience Officer (CXO) – needs to sit at the highest level of the organisation, alongside the heads of finance and operations. Often we find that the customer experience team, where they do exist, is within marketing. This is back to front: marketing is a sub-section of the overall customer experience, not the other way around, and the organisational structure should reflect this. Without this person in place, it will be very difficult to create the consistency along the customer journey that is the hallmark of a great customer experience.

Reset expectations as early as possible

Situations change, unforeseen complications arise, and people make mistakes. When this happens, our expectations need to be reset as soon as is possible. It is usually my experience that people don't mind if something goes awry, as long as they are put in a position where they can plan accordingly. This is why the waiter tells you when you sit down to eat if an item on the menu is unavailable, rather than waiting for you to try to order it.

Poor expectation management is not only a huge problem for customers, it's often a disaster for the project managers that try to deliver improvements. Humans are pretty poor at estimating how long a project will take, and failure to reset expectations about delivery dates, timelines and costs cripples a business's ability to plan and deliver a strategy. Here's how it happens: a project scope is decided upon, representatives from IT, design and project management gather to provide time and cost estimates, which are almost always wildly optimistic.

The problem is that these estimates become *commitments*. The expectations are set. Very soon it becomes obvious to everyone that the timeline is way out – they need to de-scope some elements of the project, ask for more money, or push back the deadline. Management need to be told as soon as possible that their expectations are now totally divorced from reality, but this doesn't happen because whoever made the estimates doesn't want to look like an idiot. The project carries on until it gets to just before the delivery date when all of a sudden someone confesses to the bosses that they haven't a hope of delivering anything on time. By this point they are past the point of no return and one of three things happens: they rush it out to market when it isn't finished; they reluctantly continue throwing good money after bad; or they bin the project and accept that they've just wasted a load of resources getting nowhere.

This is clearly not in anyone's interest – the customer suffers, it undermines the hard work of the team and it diminishes the likelihood of profit – yet it is commonplace. Don't punish yourselves or your customers. Ask yourself *'When things change, are we resetting expectations as soon as possible?'*

Exceed with caution

We owe much of our success as a species to an amazing ability to adapt. Almost anything can become 'normal' over time and our appreciation tends to diminish respectively. While the adage 'you don't know what you've got until it's gone' may hold true, the maxim 'under promise and over deliver' is bad advice. Continually exceeding expectations makes this an expectation in itself – one that becomes impossible to satisfy.

Expectations are continually rising as it is – we find ourselves on the *hedonic treadmill* where pleasures that were once incomparable become ordinary. To attempt continually to exceed expectations only serves to make a rod for your own back. If I reply to a client e-mail at the weekend as a one-off it may exceed expectations. If I do it habitually it is no longer the exception, it is the rule.

This presents something of a paradox. A positive surprise caused by exceeding expectations can make an experience much more pleasurable, yet to continuously exceed expectations is unsustainable. The solution is to exceed expectations in an apparently random or at least variable way, or simply as and when the opportunity presents itself. This avoids the experience feeling mechanical or contrived. Surprise is the key word here – if it's expected it's not a surprise!

In my experience, simply using the principles in this book often generates design solutions that have a tendency to surprise – neat ways of doing things that are unexpectedly pleasurable are more than enough, in fact it's often the small things that count the most. I would focus efforts on eliminating the effects of *incongruence*, *absence* and *inference* before trying to exceed expectations. In a world where expectations are so poorly managed often meeting them well is more than enough. As a final word of caution, when seeking to surprise the customer, make absolutely sure it will be a welcome surprise. You may think you are doing something nice or helpful but end up doing the opposite. Ask yourself *'What opportunities are there for a positive surprise in this experience? How can we make this personal to the customer?'*

The element of surprise – Pret A Manger

Every now and then when buying a coffee from Pret, they give it to me for free. It has happened a few times over the last few years, too often for it to be a co-incidence, yet so infrequent that it is unexpected. This makes me feel valued as a customer, puts a smile on my face and encourages me to visit again.

Re-use learnt behaviours

When considering a stage of the experience, think carefully about what behaviours may already be familiar to the customer, and whether or not they can be re-used to make the interaction feel more intuitive. Ask yourself *'What learnt behaviours apply to this situation? Are we using them effectively?'*

Learnt behaviours – Nintendo Wii

The power of learnt behaviours is clearly demonstrated by the Nintendo Wii, a games console that uses familiar gestures – you swing the control to play tennis, or punch with it when playing a boxing game – rather than the traditional buttons on a keypad. The console, launched at approximately the same time as the PlayStation 3, had sold over double that of its competitor by mid-2008.[8] By 2009 it had sold 50 million units and become the fastest selling console in history.[9]

Recognition over recall

A good rule of thumb is to try to create interactions that rely on recognition rather than recall. The more intuitive something is to use, often the more readily we adopt it. The gestural interfaces used on touch-screen smart-phones are a good example. It feels natural to swish up or down with a finger to scroll, or pinch to zoom out. Ask yourself *'How can we make this step more intuitive for the customer?'*

Intuition – the Dyson Airblade

Who would have thought that using a bathroom hand drier could become a great experience? While the Airblade could be used as an example of any number of experience design principles – sensory pleasure, effort reduction, attention to detail and clear brand values among others – whenever I use one I am struck by how *right* it feels, especially when compared to the usual hot air blowers. You just stick your hands in the opening and feel the air scrape the water off your hands like a windscreen wiper as you move them through the airflow. If a company can transform the process of drying your hands into a great experience just think what you could do. Opportunities really are everywhere!

Conventions are your friend

Conventions can become so firmly entrenched in our psyche that even if a re-design were to improve things, customer acceptance would be low. The QWERTY keyboard was originally designed to prevent typewriters from jamming, not to be the fastest possible layout, and despite alternative designs proposed over the years, claiming greater efficiency and improved ergonomics, none has achieved widespread adoption. This is no surprise – we would all have to re-learn how to type to adopt another layout. Conventions are also apparent in interface design, especially within e-commerce websites. We naturally look for terms like 'add to basket' or a small shopping trolley icon when trying to buy, and are familiar with filling out the requisite forms for address, or card details.

It is prudent to consider what existing conventions relate to your offerings, so any risk attached to changing them can be identified. Defying them unnecessarily tends to be gimmickry rather than innovation. Ask yourself *'What conventions come into play during this stage of the experience?'* When you have identified the conventions ask yourself *'Is an alternative approach genuinely better? Is resistance likely to be high? Does the benefit of learning a new approach outweigh the cost of having to learn something new?'*

The invisible solution – Dropbox

I have a laptop and a desktop computer, and often find myself needing to share files between them and with other people in my team. Until I discovered Dropbox, I used to mess around with USB sticks, intranets, or e-mailing files to myself or others to make sure I had them where I needed them. Dropbox takes this problem away by allowing you to store files in a shared folder that syncs across different devices. What makes the solution so great is that all you need to know is how to put a file in a folder. Their design just re-uses the operating system's conventions. The result is a solution that is so well integrated into our usual computing habits that it's almost invisible. Problem solved.

Take advantage of association by borrowing cues

Car designers are famous for building associations by borrowing characteristics from other products, from the fins on the back of an old Cadillac to the Lamborghini Reventon which uses cues from fighter jets to evoke the same associations of speed, power and advanced technology. Watch manufacturers are another example, often taking cues from both motorsport and aviation.

Associations can be a powerful tool to help re-frame the customer experience in a different light. Perhaps we could borrow cues from a positive experience, such as entering an exclusive club or event to transform passing through airport security from an invasive, unpleasant experience into one that conferred status on the passenger. How could we make the passenger feel like a VIP instead of a criminal? We could replace the usual crowd-control retractable belt barriers with more attractive roped ones. We could try using a red carpet instead of the dull grey one to evoke the association with entering an exclusive venue. Perhaps if the staff were smartly attired, welcoming and polite like a doorman at an up-market hotel we would feel better about the whole experience. Combined with the free water at the end, this would add up to a much improved experience. If they can have dedicated lanes for certain airlines they can certainly make those lanes more attractive. I want to fly with the airline that shows that they care about their customers and wants to do something to make the experience better. I can only imagine customers from another security lane looking on jealously and thinking – 'I'll fly with *that* airline next time.'

The power of association – Laundry Republic

Award winning dry-cleaners Laundry Republic model parts of their experience on that of luxury clothes stores. Using the same style of packaging as fashion retailers makes customers feel more like they are getting new clothes than just their old ones back – a far more pleasurable experience.

Summary

- Expectations are fundamental to how the brain works. The dopamine neurons in our brain trigger emotions based on predictions.

- Since our memories of past experiences are used to set expectations for the future, the memories we have of a customer experience are crucial.

- Over time we develop learnt behaviours and associations which can be used to our advantage.

- Expectations are powerful *and* often poorly handled, making expectation management a golden opportunity for creating a competitor advantage.

- To provide a great experience, we need to see the customer experience as one long journey, and a continuous process of *setting* and *meeting* expectations.

- Issues around expectations usually fall into three categories: *dissonance* – where expectations do not match reality; *absence* – where expectations are not set at all; and *inference* – where a customer's expectations are being set by something out of our control.

- To set more accurate expectations, and build brand trust, work on creating a consistent customer experience.

- Somebody at the highest level of the organisation needs to be responsible for the customer experience to make sure consistent expectations are set along the whole customer journey.

8

Great customer experiences are effortless

Interactions that put the onus on the customer, soaking up their time and energy, are quickly put off or replaced with those that are less demanding. Few things generate more goodwill and repeat business than being effortless to deal with. In this chapter we will cover the most useful, practical ways that you can improve the customer experience by reducing the burden of effort put on the customer at each step of the journey.

Perfection is achieved, not when there is nothing more to add, but when there is nothing left to take away.

ANTOINE DE SAINT-EXUPÉRY

Whatever the stock market does, whatever style may be fashionable, there is one trend that will not change: we will always seek to do more with less effort. Even those who want to test their endurance to the limit demand equipment that is lighter or faster to get them across the finish line first.

Technology exists to make our lives easier. If you are not constantly striving to reduce the effort required by your customer, you are easy pickings for a competitor. Even if no direct competitor sets up shop, technological developments will run you out of business. My local bike shop recently closed down, and when I asked the owner what happened he told me, 'The Internet happened.' Well it didn't happen yesterday, that's for sure. What really happened was that he chose not to respond to the advances in technology, and he chose to keep his business in a wholly inconvenient location. More people are cycling than ever, and by contrast the shop in the next town is doing well.

Let's start by considering three basic things that you can focus on to reduce the effort required from the customer:

1 *Time on task* – by reducing the amount of time a customer spends on a task, all other things being equal, you reduce the amount of effort involved.

2 *Convenience* – great products and services fit seamlessly into the customer's life: convenience is king.

3 *Simplicity* – everybody benefits from simplicity: novices, expert users, and the company behind the offering. The more straightforward a product or service is to use, the less physical and mental effort is required.

These serve as excellent high-level rules of thumb to refer back to. The following general guidelines are all combinations of these three principles and, while by no means exhaustive, should provide a good starting point for reducing the effort required on the part of the customer.

- Less, but better
- Prioritise
- Limit choices to a manageable number
- Reduce time on task
- Reduce wait times
- Reduce the possibility for error
- Use convenient channels
- Be in the right place, at the right time
- Speak the customer's language

Less, but better

Dieter Rams, whose minimalist designs for Braun are a clear influence on Apple, wrote that 'Good design is as little design as possible.'[1] He even called his book about design at Braun *Less, But Better*.[2] The simpler something is, the less effort is required. The most fundamental way to do this is what John Maeda, author of *The Laws of Simplicity*, calls 'thoughtful reduction'.[3] There are three things in particular that we should strive to reduce.

1 FEATURES

In Chapter 5 we explored how continually adding features to a product can have a detrimental effect. The more features there are the more expensive it gets to add new ones, the more it costs to maintain, and usually the slower the performance. At the same time it becomes more difficult to use. Also, the longer your feature list at the start of the project, the more expensive and time consuming it will be to bring it to market. Ask yourself 'What are the non-essential features? Can we remove them?' Remember, if they really are great features you can add them in later.

Less but better – WriteRoom

I am writing this book on a word processor called WriteRoom. It has almost no features, just a green cursor on a full black screen. With no intrusive navigation, menus or options I can better concentrate on what's important to me: turning my thinking into words.

2 TASKS

If the consumer has a clear goal in mind, it can be helpful to frame each action required as a barrier to completion. Using the set of stages and steps you have identified, start looking for ways in which the list can be pruned. Ask yourself 'Are there opportunities to do the task on behalf of the customer? Can we de-duplicate any data entry tasks? Can tasks be combined? Could a step be automated so the customer doesn't need to do it?'

Reducing switching penalties – First Direct

If you set up a new current account with the bank First Direct, their 'EasySwitch' team takes care of the tiresome admin for you, moving over direct debits and standing orders and setting up the text message banking for you.

Effortless set up – Vodafone Red Box

A major frustration with setting up a new phone is copying over your contacts. Vodafone now offer a service that does this for you in their stores.

Task consolidation – Joseph Joseph

Kitchen and cookware brand Joseph Joseph make a range of wonderfully innovative products that help reduce effort by supporting multiple tasks, like the 'Chop2Pot' hinged chopping boards that form a chute when you squeeze the handle so you can guide the food straight into a container or pan, and the 'Rinse&Chop' which combines a chopping board and strainer. Joseph Joseph have become one of the fastest growing companies in their market. Opportunities to reduce effort are everywhere!

3 WORDS

Consider this extract from *The Elements of Style*: 'Omit needless words. Vigorous writing is concise. A sentence should contain no unnecessary words, a paragraph no unnecessary sentences, for the same reason that a drawing should have no unnecessary lines and a machine no unnecessary parts.'[4] This is easier said than done, but worth the effort. Where instructions are necessary, make them clear and concise. Where a customer requires information, get them to the facts. When faced with the task of writing something, ask yourself *'How can I communicate this clearly and concisely?'*

Omit needless words – rework

This business book shrunk from 52,000 to 27,000 words during editing. It gets the reader straight to the good stuff, and because it is so short it is more likely to be read in its entirety. The result: a best-seller in both the UK and USA.

Prioritise

Even after pruning the features and tasks, it is likely that there will be a lot left. This is fine. You can still make a feature-rich experience effortless by *prioritising*. In almost every product or service there is a core set of tasks that everybody uses. By making these as effortless to use as possible, everybody benefits. You can work your way through the list to the more advanced features over time. In *The Simplicity Shift*, Scott Jenson provides a simple technique to prioritise a task or feature list:[5] using the consolidated list of steps that you have created, or a feature list if you have one, rank the items on the list in the following two ways, from the perspective of your customer profiles.

1 How frequently the task will be done/feature will be used – rarely (1), moderately (2), frequently (3).

2 How important it is to the product or service – low (1), useful (2), critical (3).

Once you've got this, use the following process to prioritise your tasks:

- *Force an even distribution* – if there are 12 features for example, only allow four in each category.
- *Add together the rankings* – e.g. if a feature or task is frequent (3) and critical (3) it gets 6.
- *Order the features or tasks by their total score* – this is your prioritised list.
- *Get to work on the top third of the list.*[6]

This is a very worthwhile exercise since it will force you to focus on what is most important in your product or service. We rarely get the time or budget to do everything we'd like, but this is no bad thing. Constraints can force us to come up with much better solutions. As the great designer Charles Eames once said, 'I have never been forced to accept compromises, but I have willingly accepted constraints.'[7] Try to look at these constraints in a positive rather than negative way, as challenges to be overcome rather than barriers to success. They are an inevitable part of life.

Limit choices to a manageable number

In the early 2000s few brands made a compelling argument for simplicity like Nokia. My friends and I all had Nokia phones and we loved that you could pick up any model and be able to use it straight away. Scott Jenson's book *The Simplicity Shift* even used them as a case study for how simplicity can drive success in the marketplace.[8]

Nowadays Nokia are more likely to be a case study of what not to do. At the time of writing their website offers 25 models, and if I narrow it down to just touch-screen smart-phones there are still 14 to choose from.[9] The Lumia 710, 800 or 900; the 808, the E7-00, E6-00 ... I give up. There is no immediately visible difference between them and the naming is totally arbitrary. The onus is on me to research them. Who can be bothered?

The more choice there is, the greater the effort required to decide on a course of action. This applies to everything from choosing which product to buy in the first place, right down to choosing options from a settings menu on the phone we do end up with. Assuming that we have already reduced the product and service as well as we can, and have prioritised what remains, there are four further techniques we can use to reduce the burden of choice.

1 PROGRESSIVE DISCLOSURE

This technique involves separating information out into different layers then showing only what is relevant at that time.[10] A common example is menu systems on websites or computers, where rather than showing every option at once, you choose from one list, then another – the options are revealed progressively to keep the volume manageable. This technique can dramatically reduce the burden of choice, the likelihood of error and improve learning efficiency.

2 THE FIVE HAT RACKS

This model, like progressive disclosure, is a wonderful nugget from the book *Universal Principles of Design* which I highly recommend. The five hat racks refers to five ways in which information can be organised: *category, time, location, alphabet,* and *continuum.* We could order a list of books for sale by *category,* such as business books or fiction books; by *time,* such as date of release; by *location* – of publisher, author or subject matter; *alphabetically,* by author name or title; or along another *continuum* – highest-rated or best-selling for example.[11] Where there are multiple options, organising them in a way that makes sense to the customer will make choosing easier. Ask yourself *'How should this information be organised?'*

3 THE ONE RIGHT WAY

Flexibility is the enemy of simplicity. To create a great customer experience we must balance the customer's need for control and freedom of choice with the need for simplicity. There may be a variety of ways to perform a given task, and the temptation may be to cater for all of them – in a store, on the website, over the phone, with an app. You may end up creating unnecessary work for yourself. If you design a web-based solution that is good enough, you may find that the staff in the store and call centre can use it too. It may even work well enough on a phone-sized screen that you needn't ship the feature as part of an app. You may find that 98 per cent of customers use the same method. Don't let the tail wag the dog by expending unnecessary resources on a tiny minority. Ask yourself *'Is there one right way of doing this task?'*

4 OMAKASE

This Japanese phrase, often used in sushi restaurants, means 'I'll leave it to you'.[12] The customer delegates decision making to the chef, taking away the burden of choice entirely. I often wish I had to make fewer decisions in life, and have never struggled with delegating tasks where it will free up my time. As a keen photographer I often get pictures framed to put up in the house, and have used one local framer exclusively for years. He has visited me to drop off pictures and knows the decor of the house well. For the last year or two, whenever I drop off anything new I leave it up to him to decide what will best complement the picture and the environment in which it will be hung. I could spend endless hours fussing over different finishes, mounting styles and fixings. Why not leave it to the expert? I for one wish there were more opportunities for Omakase. Ask yourself 'Should we offer to decide for the customer?'

Omakase – iPod shuffle

For anyone with a large music collection, deciding what to listen to can be a challenge, so we often tend to end up listening to the same things over and over. The shuffle function on the iPod makes it easy by playing random tracks from your library. It's a great way to rediscover forgotten favourites, and if you aren't in the mood you just press next.

Reduce time on task

Even after giving our task list a thorough pruning, doing what we can to consolidate, automate and otherwise reduce the burden on the customer, we will likely still be left with a lot of tasks. Using your prioritised list, starting with the most frequently used and critical tasks first, find ways to make these tasks as simple and efficient as possible. Often all it takes to come up with ideas is to think actively about them in the first place. Ask yourself 'What would make this task quicker and easier for the customer?'

Streamlining repetitive tasks – Ringo Mobile Parking

This mobile parking system is well designed. It remembers the vehicle registrations for multiple vehicles, the locations you parked at recently and your bank details. To pay for parking at my local railway station I use the keypad to enter the number of days I wish to park for, then confirm payment using just the three digits from the back of the debit card.

Reduce wait times

Nobody likes to be kept waiting. It feels like a waste of time, and can be extremely frustrating. When mapping out the stages and steps of the customer experience I suggested noting down wait times as their own steps. Now it's time to see how we can reduce the impact of these flat spots on the customer experience using four techniques.

1 ROOT CAUSE ANALYSIS

Nobody designs an experience to keep people waiting around. It's a symptom of some other issue: slow servers, increased demand for the service, not enough staff, poor process design. Whenever wait times crop up, ask yourself *'Why does the customer have to wait? What is the root cause? How can it be reduced or removed entirely?'*

Reduced wait times – Kwik Fit Car Insurance

Car insurance company Kwik Fit has a free callback service that will hold your place in the queue. The service is activated when you call them, so they already have your phone number; all you do is say your name and confirm the number was correct, then hang up and get on with something else.

2 RE-SEQUENCING

We are often able to eliminate wait times by doing tasks in a different order such that the dead time is used up on another activity. Ask yourself *'How can we re-sequence tasks to eliminate dead time?'*

3 INFORMING

If customers must be kept waiting, it helps to keep them informed of progress. (The importance of this kind of feedback is discussed more thoroughly in the next chapter.) Ask yourself *'How can we keep the customer informed about how long they will be waiting?'*

4 ALLEVIATING THE BOREDOM

Waiting around is boring. If you know that the customer is likely to be waiting around, try to make that wait as pleasant as possible.

A fun distraction

One coffee shop I saw in New Zealand had a lemon floating in a tub of water on the counter where you waited for your drink. If you could get a dollar coin to balance on the lemon without it rolling into the water you got your drink for free. Opportunities are everywhere!

Reduce the possibility for error

Errors create re-work, which increases the effort involved to complete a given task. Minimise errors by preventing them where possible. If it is not possible to prevent an error from occurring, put in place means to detect the error promptly and help the customer recover from the error as quickly and easily as possible. The topic of errors is covered in far more detail in the next chapter.

Use convenient channels

The excitement around multi-channel customer experiences is caused by their potential to increase customer satisfaction through convenience. Click and collect and online check-in are both good examples. The question you should ask yourself is 'Which channel or touchpoint is most convenient for the customer to perform this task?' Remember, multi-channel isn't the same as omni-channel. The key is to identify which channel or touchpoint is most appropriate.

Channel appropriateness – NHS Direct

NHS Direct is an excellent free service available in the UK where you can call to speak to a nurse if you are feeling unwell, who can advise you as to how serious the symptoms are, and a suitable course of action. This reduces the burden of unnecessary appointments at doctors' surgeries, while being more convenient for citizens who may otherwise have to make an appointment and visit the doctor only to be told they need some rest. At the other end of the scale, if you really are unwell they can call an ambulance for you.

Be in the right place at the right time

Somebody once told me a well-designed product or service was like a good waiter: attentive, polite, but unobtrusive when not needed. To do this, a waiter must be in the right place at the right time to provide the service you require. The joy of online shopping is that it is always open. The same is often not true of shops or call centres. Ask yourself *'Are we available to serve customers at times that suit them?'* If you have a physical presence, ask yourself *'Are we conveniently located for our customers?'*

Speak the customer's language

Half of the problem in the example from Nokia earlier in this chapter is the naming of the products: they are neither memorable, nor do they reveal any useful information about the product. This is part of a broader problem in business. Time after time I find myself repelled by unfamiliar acronyms, technical jargon and marketing nonsense. There is no quicker way to alienate and infuriate your customer. Ask yourself *'Are we speaking the language of the customer?'*

Getting it right – Amazon

No discussion of effortless customer experiences would be complete without a mention of the online retailer Amazon, whose attention to detail and systematic reduction of effort has been a

▶

significant contributor to their success. Their patented one-click shopping system, as the name suggests, allows the customer to buy a product using just one click of the mouse. Wishlists, customer reviews and recommendations all make deciding what to buy easier. They have extended this approach to their e-book reader, the Kindle. Their website boasts that you can be reading a book within 60 seconds of ordering it, and that the battery lasts for up to a month[12] – great examples of reducing wait times, channel convenience, and eliminating repetition in action.

The 3G service to download contents to a Kindle e-book reader comes fully set up with no bills or commitments, eliminating yet more tiresome tasks. It is no surprise that when we think of online shopping most of us think first of Amazon. They have even made returning goods as simple as possible, something that is often problematic for online retailers.

Summary

- We always want to do more with less effort.

- Technology exists to make our lives easier.

- To reduce effort, consider three parameters: time on task, convenience, and simplicity.

- Reduce features and tasks, and omit unnecessary words. Remember: *less, but better.*

- Prioritise tasks and features so that the most frequently used and important ones can be made as effortless as possible.

- Reduce the effort required when making decisions by limiting choices to a manageable number.

- Streamlining tasks means less effort is needed to reach the customer's goal.

- Reduce wait times where possible.

- Errors create re-work. Eliminate them where possible.

- Use convenient channels.

- Convenience is serving the customer in the right place at the right time.

- Speak the customer's language.

9

Great customer experiences are stress free

We instinctively avoid stressful situations. Customer experiences that eliminate confusion, uncertainty and anxiety reap the rewards, generating a competitive advantage, loyalty and a peerless brand image. This chapter explores common causes of stress during customer experiences, and what you can do to minimise their effects.

Confusion is the chief cause of worry. HERBERT E. HAWKES

Most people have unwanted stress in their lives. We are stressed at work, stressed at home; many find it stressful trying to get home from work. It is easy to see how the products and services that we interact with contribute to this stress. We are often confronted by products that are confusing to operate; computers crash unpredictably; we call customer service teams who can't or won't help us. The sheer volume of information we are presented with and the number of decisions we need to make day-to-day can leave us feeling exhausted. When we go shopping we often have so much choice we become paralysed by indecision.

How we respond to these stressors in our environment is very much down to the individual, and the emphasis is on ways to cope better. We can buy books like *Stress-proof Your Life*, or the wonderfully titled *Stress Buster: How To Stop Stress From Killing You*. But why emphasise a cure rather than a prevention? The reason is that the sources of stress are usually out of our control. I don't decide whether the trains run on time, or how many varieties of beans there are for sale at the supermarket.

The people who can remove these sources of stress are in the businesses that create the products and services we use. The main reason why so many products and services are stressful to use is simply because *they were never designed to be stress free*. Nobody ever actually asked the question, 'How might this interaction cause stress for the customer and what can we do to reduce that?' Of course, nobody designed them *to be* stressful either, it just seeps in wherever you *don't* prevent it. The more stressful our lives get, the more we appreciate those customer experiences that offer us a time-out. A stressless customer experience is a major competitive advantage. It's also relatively easy to do.

There are situations where stress is taken extremely seriously, typically in environments where performance is critical to safety – aviation, combat or nuclear power plants – and because of this there is a wealth of literature on the topic. The principles that human factors experts and psychologists rely on when designing for these high consequence environments can be put to work to improve any customer experience – we are all human, whether we are flying a jet or buying a mobile phone.

The rest of this chapter tells you how to do this in practice, so you can make your products and services as stressless as possible for the customer. I start by discussing errors as a source of stress that warrants special attention, before moving on to some more general guidelines.

Errors

I thought long and hard about whether the subject of error belonged within this chapter on stress or the previous chapter on effort since it relates to both. Errors create re-work which requires more effort, but the relationship between errors and stress is stronger since it is reinforcing: stress can lead to errors, errors can lead to stress. That the subject of error relates to both principles makes it all the more important, so it is worth considering in detail.

Errors are a daily consequence for all of us, most of which are small and insignificant: typos, forgetting things, taking a wrong turn when driving. There are also those that have devastating consequences. To err is human, and although we can never eliminate error completely, what we can do is design customer experiences that reduce the likelihood of errors occurring in the first place, and where a prevention is not possible, allow us to recover gracefully when they do happen.

Poka yoke

This two pronged approach – prevention and detection – is known as *poka yoke* or 'mistake proofing' in lean production and management theory, and forms part of the zero quality control manufacturing method. Examples of poka yoke in practice include:

- Sim cards that can only be inserted the correct way
- The hole at the top of the sink that drains water away to prevent overflowing
- Fuel pumps where the diesel nozzle won't fit in a petrol tank

To put poka yoke to work for your customer experience, all you need to do is select a *stage* or *step* from the customer journey and generate a list of the possible mistakes a customer might make, and then come up with ways that this mistake might be *prevented* or if prevention is not possible, *detected and recovered*.

Let's consider the errors the customer might make during a seemingly trivial part of the air travel experience: packing for their trip. Errors that relate to packing that I have made myself include:

- Forgetting something – passport, boarding card, toothbrush, items of clothing, or my own bug bear, the adapter for foreign power sockets
- Packing inappropriately for the weather at my destination
- Exceeding the weight limit
- Taking fragile items that I cannot take into the cabin, such as a musical instrument
- Taking a hand luggage bag that is too big for the overhead locker
- Carrying items in hand luggage that contravene security measures – fluids or cosmetics

There are many potential solutions to these errors. When it comes to forgetting things, detection can either happen at security or check-in if we've forgotten our passport, but may go undetected until we unpack at the other end. Either way it's too late, so we should focus on prevention.

One way might be to send an e-mail out to the customer with a 'top ten forgotten items' to raise awareness. Another more fun solution might be to post the customer a re-usable hanger to put on the inside handle of the front door like the Do Not Disturb signs you get in hotels, that say, *'Don't forget the: ...'* with a blank space for you to write in your own items. This could be re-used for any number of things and might be a nice way to keep the brand in front of the customer.

When it comes to exceeding the weight limit, again prevention is better so that the customer doesn't get charged for excess baggage. A simple solution might just be clearer communication about what the limits are (in kilograms, stones and pounds) so the customer can weigh their bags on the bathroom scales before they go. Another helpful solution might be to provide the customer with a list of the shops at the departure and arrival airports, with a message along the lines of 'Not sure whether to pack it? Here are the shops you'll be passing.'

To prevent packing inappropriately for the weather, we could use the outbound and return flight dates and destination to provide a personal weather forecast for the customer before they fly – another way to be helpful, and another way to stand out. Doing this basic error prevention and detection activity for each stage of the customer experience should open up opportunities for improvements that you had never considered before. There is a worksheet available on my website, at www.mattwatkinson.co.uk/worksheets, that you can use to help with this.

Error classification

Such is the variance in error types, causes and consequences that to make this task approachable it helps to have a way of classifying these errors. James Reason, whose books on human error are the gold standard, provides such a framework. I have condensed the key themes.

A basic distinction is between errors where our *intentions* were wrong, and errors where our *actions* were wrong. An incorrect action but a *correct intention* is if I put the milk in the cupboard instead of the fridge if I'm half asleep. A correct action but an *incorrect intention* is when I take a left turn successfully at a junction when driving, only to realise later that I needed to turn right. This gives rise to three simple categories that we can use to help us identify possible errors that a customer might make: *knowledge-based mistakes* (which relate to intentions), and *slips* and *lapses* (which relate to actions).[1]

KNOWLEDGE-BASED MISTAKES

These occur when the customer has inadequate information or expertise to deal with a situation. It is easy to make mistakes when we don't know what we are doing. A common example would be buying a product or service that doesn't suit our needs in the first place. Knowledge-based errors are especially common in situations where there is an over-abundance of choice, or where we have little experience. To discover these mistakes, ask yourself *'Does the customer have the information or expertise to complete this stage or step successfully?'*

SLIPS

These are the most common type of error. Typos, dropping something or turning on the indicators in the car instead of the windscreen wipers. Slips have the advantage of normally being quite easy to detect and observe and thus can be picked up quite quickly in testing.

LAPSES

Lapses relate mostly to forgetfulness. To discover lapses, ask yourself *'What might a customer forget that will prevent them from completing the task? Is there a part of a sequence that a customer might miss out by accident that will lead to an error?'* Examples include missing a field when completing a form online, forgetting a password or, as we saw above, forgetting that pesky foreign power adapter.

Prioritising errors

We may discover so many possible errors across the customer journey that we cannot possibly deal with them all. Drawing again on James Reason's work, there are four characteristics that we can use to prioritise errors:[2]

1 Frequency – *How likely is this error to occur?*

2 Cost – *How severe is the outcome of this error – is it a 'free lesson' or likely to result in death, financial loss or damage to other assets?*

3 Ease of detection – *Can this error be identified quickly and easily?*

4 Ease of recovery – *Is this a simple error to prevent? Is it easy to reverse?*

We might find that there are one or two high frequency errors that come at a considerable cost for the customer. If so, focus on solving these first, then tackle those low frequency errors that are easy to detect and recover from last.

Guidelines for error management and stress reduction

Many of the guidelines that are of specific use within the context of error management are also applicable in a more general sense for reducing the stress a customer might experience. There is a stress worksheet available on my website, at www.mattwatkinson.co.uk/worksheets, that will help put these into practice. There are seven guidelines:

1 Consider the customer's competence

2 Limit choices to a manageable number

3 Make options distinctive

4 Let the customer undo their mistakes

5 Clarify the reason for the task

6 Provide frequent and responsive feedback

7 Consider any distractions in the environment

1 CONSIDER THE CUSTOMER'S COMPETENCE

Our competence affects how stressful we find a task and how likely we are to make mistakes. Writing in *Engineering Psychology and Human Performance*, Wickens and Hollands explain that experts are less likely to get flustered than novices for three reasons. First, as our skills develop we become able to perform tasks without consciously thinking about them, which frees up more mental resources to combat stressors. Second, an expert will likely have a broader range of strategies available to them to perform a given task, so they can change tack to get to the result they need. Finally, greater experience often involves greater familiarity with the stressors that are involved in that task, and so the operator is better able to cope with them.[3]

The key thing is to design an experience that is *appropriate for the customer's level of competence*. This is something that computer games designers are excellent at. The first level of a game is always easy enough for a novice to enjoy, then the levels become progressively more difficult to challenge the player as their competence develops.

When looking at the customer experience ask yourself whether there is a variation in levels of competence among your customers. If there is, consider the optimum solutions for these different competence levels, so that neither the novice nor the expert is penalised. This may be something as simple as providing hints for the novice that can be switched off for the expert, or having an advanced menu option. Another option may be to allow the customer to specify their level of expertise. For online supermarkets, when looking at the recipes they offer for inspiration, they usually do not allow the user to specify their level of expertise. They incorrectly assume that the customer knows the techniques required and what the ingredients are. For a given stage, ask yourself *'How can we make the experience appropriate for the customer's level of competence?'*

2 LIMIT CHOICES TO A MANAGEABLE NUMBER

We touched on this topic in the previous chapter on effort, since the more choice there is the greater effort is required to choose. Let's look at it again, since an abundance of choice can also create stress. Having choice is undoubtedly a good thing. It is inseparable from the ideal of freedom, and fundamental to our most basic need to feel in control of our lives. This does not mean that *more* choice is always *better*. As Barry Schwartz explains in *The Paradox of Choice,* the opposite is often true:

> *As the number of choices keeps growing, negative aspects of having a multitude of options begin to appear. As the number of choices grows further, the negatives escalate until we become overloaded. At this point, choice no longer liberates, but debilitates ... It means that decisions require more effort. It makes mistakes more likely. It makes the psychological consequences of mistakes more severe ... there comes a point at which opportunities become so numerous that we feel overwhelmed. Instead of feeling in control we feel unable to cope.*[4]

We have all experienced this feeling at some point. The more important the decision is – buying a house for example – the more stressful the decision becomes. There is not just choosing the property, there is choosing the kind of mortgage you want, then the specific mortgage deal. All these choices make for a very stressful experience.

One solution is to reduce the number of options available to a customer at any step in the experience. For a given stage of the experience, ask yourself *'Is the amount of choice at this point likely to overwhelm the customer? What can we do to make this more manageable?'*

Making choice manageable – Nike ID

The Nike ID website allows you to order customised Nike products, specifying combinations of colours, and materials. The possibilities are endless, and this can be quite a daunting task. When they first launched this service I went online to have a go at designing my own, but quickly found myself overwhelmed by the options. Nike have improved the service over the years, specifically tackling this problem by allowing the customer to start with some basic combinations or designs from other customers rather than a blank canvas. This makes the process of customising your trainers much less stressful.

3 MAKE OPTIONS DISTINCTIVE

The stress caused by an abundance of choice is lessened if the differences between the options are clear. It is with that in mind that I am recoiling in horror from the website of my local rail operator. If I choose to buy a 'leisure ticket' as opposed to a 'business ticket' I am now able to choose between off-peak, super off-peak, off-peak day, or ranger and rover tickets. What are the off-peak hours? They are not provided anywhere on the page. How am I to decide between them?

It is no surprise that when I get the train home from London, almost without fail somebody is found to have the wrong ticket and forced to endure the embarrassment of having the ticket inspector explain what they did wrong in front of a carriage full of people, before charging them for a new ticket. This must be a nightmare for tourists. To prevent this problem, when evaluating a stage or step of a customer experience, ask yourself *'Are the differences between options clear?'*

4 LET THE CUSTOMER UNDO THEIR MISTAKES

Learning something new is often a process of trial and error. The key is to allow customers to recover from these errors as quickly and easily as possible. Slips and lapses are an everyday part of life, so try to design a customer experience that is forgiving. When you have your list of possible errors for a given stage or step, ask yourself *'How can we make this error easy to recover from?'*

> ## Undo – Gmail
> One thing I have always liked about Gmail is the undo function that appears at the top of the screen when you perform an action such as deleting an e-mail. This allows you to get on with things in the knowledge that if you slip up you can quickly and easily recover from it.

5 CLARIFY THE REASON FOR THE TASK

We are often required to perform tasks where the reason or benefit is unclear. We find ourselves asking *'Why do you need this information?'* or *'Why do I need to do things in this order?'* There are usually sound reasons for why these tasks must be performed, but when we are left in the dark it can make us anxious or reluctant to cooperate. When working on a stage of the customer experience, ask yourself *'Is the reason for completing this task clear to the customer?'* In most cases it will be obvious, but sometimes an explanation might help.

6 PROVIDE FREQUENT AND RESPONSIVE FEEDBACK

In his classic book *How to Stop Worrying and Start Living*, Dale Carnegie describes how half the worry in the world is caused by trying to make decisions without the necessary facts.[5] Many people fear the unknown – uncertainty makes us anxious. The solution to this is to provide the customer with frequent and responsive feedback to reassure them that they are progressing towards their goal, or point out deviations as soon as possible. Progress bars and confirmation e-mails are both examples of such feedback systems.

One of the worst experiences I've had as a customer in recent years was with a breakdown recovery. I sat for hours waiting for one of their fleet to arrive to repair my broken-down car feeling totally out of the loop. At first they said it would be an hour. When I called back they said it would be another hour. Eventually I waited three hours for someone to arrive. They gave me no feedback whatsoever about how things were progressing. After the second time this happened I switched to a competitor. When designing a customer interaction, ask yourself *'How can we keep the customer well-informed of their progress towards their goal? Do we provide adequate feedback that they have successfully completed a task? How quickly is this feedback provided?'*

7 CONSIDER ANY DISTRACTIONS IN THE ENVIRONMENT

The world is full of distractions that can draw our attention away from a task at hand. Interruptions can cause us to lose our place and make mistakes. Background noise can hinder concentration. When in an emotional state, we can find ourselves unable to focus at all. In short, the *context* in which an experience takes place needs to be considered, or where possible experienced first hand. This is what many researchers and human factors specialists spend their time doing, especially for high consequence environments such as combat or surgery.

Distractions are everywhere, so they must be considered: is the customer doing a task online and likely to be distracted by e-mail, instant messenger or social networks? Is the task so boring the customer is likely to actively seek out distractions? Are you trying to communicate important information to a customer in a noisy, crowded shop? Is the customer under intense time pressure? Are they likely to be either too excited or too distressed to concentrate? For any stage of the experience, ask yourself *'What distractions might the customer face when performing this task? How can we bear these in mind when designing this interaction?'*

Summary

- A stressless customer experience is a major competitive advantage.

- We can use the principles that experts use for high consequence environments to improve any customer experience.

- The relationship between errors and stress is reinforcing: stress can lead to errors, errors can lead to stress.

- Identify ways that errors might be prevented or if prevention is not possible, detected and recovered.

- Errors can be classified into knowledge-based mistakes, slips and lapses.

- We can prioritise errors by frequency, cost, ease of detection and ease of recovery.

- Consider the customer's competence: novices are more likely to get flustered than experts.

- Limiting choices to a manageable number and making options distinctive reduces the stress involved in decision making.

- Design for forgiveness: let the customer undo their mistakes.

- Clarifying the reason for the task reduces uncertainty.

- Providing frequent and responsive feedback will reassure the customer that they are on the right track.

- Consider any distractions in the environment that may reduce the customer's attention on the task at hand.

10

Great customer experiences indulge the senses

From delicious food, to relaxing music or a beautiful painting, we all actively seek sensory pleasure. Customer experiences that delight the senses win our hearts and have us coming back for more. In this chapter we will explore what each sense has to offer to improve the customer experience.

We made the buttons on the screen look so good you'll want to lick them. STEVE JOBS

'Can I help you, sir?' the sales assistant asked. He'd been watching me for a while now with a slightly worried look on his face.

'No, no I'm fine. I'm just trying to find a new kettle.' Ten minutes earlier, I'd walked into the store and found myself faced with a row of 60 models, all of which I was sure were capable of boiling water. Decisions, decisions …

I started at one end and worked my way along, picking them up in turn to get a feel for the handle, then opening the lid to see how smoothly the hinge worked. Unfortunately the poor assistant had chosen to offer his services when I was barely halfway through, and now felt compelled to stand nearby, radiating awkwardness.

Five minutes later, we had a winner (or 59 losers depending on how you look at it). When I picked it up I could feel the quality immediately. It had a reassuring weight to it, and a subtle but striking stainless steel finish. 'That'll look nice in the kitchen,' I thought. The handle had a lovely rubbery feel to it, and the ON button, a rocker switch conveniently placed where the thumb falls, made a suitably chunky 'click'. I pressed the button to open the lid, and my eyes lit up like a child at Christmas. It rose before me, silent, graceful and precise, like the hatch opening on a spaceship. I smiled at my new friend, 'I'll take it!'

Design is often thought of as a 'creative profession' but to my mind it is more like a branch of applied psychology: to get the best results we need to work from the brain outwards, starting with what we want a customer to think, feel and do, then creating a solution to achieve these ends. Our senses are critical to this goal since they form the bridge between the environmental factors which we can control and the mind which we hope to influence.

Since every product or service is fundamentally a sensual experience, the way in which our senses are stimulated must always have an end in mind, and never be arbitrary or left to chance. In every interaction we recruit our senses to provide us with useful information. Think about a trip to the supermarket: we judge a product's quality by the design of packaging, and infer freshness by smell. We squeeze avocados to see if they are ripe; we can tell how fresh a celery is by how crunchy it sounds.

Beyond the functional

One of my most cherished possessions is a 1954 Jaeger Le Coultre Atmos clock: one of the great masterpieces of design and engineering of the twentieth century. The clock is powered by tiny changes in temperature and atmospheric pressure, which allows it to run perpetually in an ordinary domestic environment with no batteries or winding: a temperature change of one degree is enough to power the clock for two days.

That these clocks first went on sale in 1936 is quite surprising to many, and the design and engineering evokes a time when things were built to last. Every Atmos takes a month to build by hand, followed by five weeks of adjustment before they can be shipped. They have graced the homes of John F. Kennedy, Winston Churchill and Charlie

Chaplin among others, and were often given as retirement presents to executives.

The Atmos clock embodies everything that I consider to be excellence in design: innovation, precision, thoughtfulness down to the finest details, longevity, environmental sensitivity, and beautiful form wedded to useful function. This clock also represents to me the antithesis of the planned obsolescence that characterises modern consumer goods and is all the more appealing because of it. They were originally claimed to have a 600-year service life; however, nowadays routine maintenance is required every 20 years owing to increased pollutants in the atmosphere. I certainly hope my Atmos is still running happily in 600 years.

From a purely functional perspective, the Atmos clock does not tell the time any better than the clock on my oven. However, when they see it, visitors to my home tend to gaze in wonder at it, make cooing noises when they see the tiny cogs spinning silently, and ask where they can get one.

The lesson from this story is simple: to create a great customer experience, the sensory characteristics of a product or brand must not just play a functional role in conveying useful information to us, they must also have aesthetic appeal. The Atmos clock tells me that the time is 12:01 which is good, but it also inspires me and makes me smile, which makes it great. There is no point arguing over whether 'form or function' is more important; you can't ignore either.

Research has shown time and again that aesthetically appealing products are perceived as easier to operate, are more likely to be used and are more readily forgiven when errors occur.[1] Despite this, designers of all disciplines find themselves working tirelessly to educate their clients, who are often dismissive. This is not only a gross misunderstanding of design as a discipline, it's a fundamental misunderstanding about the nature of human beings. The things we buy reflect our identity, and we are incredibly sensitive to how our individual values, tastes and aspirations are communicated through them.

Five senses – infinite opportunities

Each sense offers an abundance of opportunities to delight the customer. By carefully considering how the senses are stimulated we can do much to increase the appeal of our products and services, and create a more pleasurable ownership experience.

Unfortunately, to cover this topic in detail is far beyond the scope of this book. I have in my office nearly a hundred books that cover just visual design; to do the other four senses justice would require hundreds more. With this in mind, I will briefly cover each sense in turn with the aim of inspiring you to think about how you might put them all to use to enhance your customer experience, then finish the chapter by providing some more general advice to help you avoid some common mistakes I've seen over the years.

VISION

Sight is the sense that receives the lion's share of attention during the design process. It is no wonder – the range of visual stimuli we can process is staggering, allowing us to discern motion, geometric properties and textures, not to mention colour, tone and brightness. The way a product looks is hugely important. You'd think that going out for dinner would be all about how the food tastes, yet how often do we choose our meal based on what looks great coming out of the kitchen on its way to someone else's table?

Advertising, interface, product and packaging design all focus great attention on the visual stimuli, perhaps because we rely heavily on our eyesight to infer other characteristics of an object from a distance: we can usually say whether something looks heavy or soft at a glance without needing to touch it, for example. The most basic question to ask yourself when trying to establish how something should look is *'What qualities of the brand or product must be conveyed through its appearance?'*

Gü Puddings – dedicated to decadence

As anyone who has tried these desserts will testify, Gü Puddings are delicious and decadent in equal measure; but where they stand out is the excellent job they have done of expressing what's inside the box on the outside of it. By setting their simple but bold logo and vibrant colours against a dark background, the result is eye-catching without being over-bearing. The glossy finish in the box oozes refinement and luxury. The packaging performs its role perfectly, seducing the customer into picking it up, at which point it's halfway into the trolley.

TOUCH

Touch is the most intimate of the senses, yet also involves the most effort since it requires direct contact with the object. Our sense of touch allows us to explore an object in an amazing variety of ways: we can discern the shape, texture, weight, hardness, size and temperature of an object all just through touching it.

This makes our sense of touch an incredibly rich medium for gaining information about a product, and it also makes the tactile properties of a product a huge opportunity for differentiation. Research also suggests that touching an object in the shop results in a greater feeling of 'psychological ownership'[2] that makes a purchase more likely. This gives us three things to focus on when considering the customer's sense of touch.

What does the customer touch? By identifying the parts of the product that the customer touches you can focus your attention where it matters. I've often thought that otherwise beautifully decorated rooms are often let down by light switches and power sockets that feel cheap and nasty. Anything the customer touches is an opportunity in waiting.

What qualities of the product must be communicated through touch? Should it be rough, smooth, warm, cold, soft, solid, rounded, angular, sleek or boxy, heavy or light? Each of these properties can be considered. We often associate quality with solidity; rounded edges lend a product an air of friendliness; clothing is often bought because it has a soft feel to the material. If something is to be transported, how can it be made lighter?

How can we seduce the customer into touching it? If the tactile properties of your product are part of its appeal, you must encourage the customer to touch the product in the first place. Don't hide it away in a glass case or wrap it up in packaging. Have a demonstration model they can play around with; better still a knowledgeable salesperson who can point out all the effort you went to to get it feeling just right.

SCENT

Scent is the most evocative sense: a smell can immediately conjure long forgotten memories and trigger powerful emotions. I once came back from the kitchen to find a friend with his nose buried in the sound hole of my classical guitar; he said the cedar wood reminded him of his grandpa's cigar boxes, and many people associate the smell of citrus with freshness and cleanliness.[3]

Despite its potential, scent is the most neglected of the senses, perhaps because there are few universally appealing smells; we also typically become acclimatised to a scent within 15 minutes[4] or so, at which point it loses its effect, unless we leave the vicinity and return again. That this is still an emerging area should not put you off considering scent as an opportunity to add something more to the experience, just make sure you test any experiments thoroughly. Ask yourself *'Could we incorporate a scent into the experience?'*

Stefan Floridian Waters – the smell of Singapore Airlines

Singapore Airlines were quite far ahead of the curve when they had a unique fragrance created for them called Stefan Floridian Waters in the late 1990s. The scent, used in cabin crews' perfume, in the hot towels and across their fleet of planes, was often immediately noticed by frequent flyers, making them feel more at home, and triggering positive memories of previous experiences with the airline.[5]

HEARING

We often have little choice over whether or not we hear something in our environment. We can close our eyes, of course, but closing our ears is pretty difficult. This can make sound one of the most intrusive elements of our environment. The implication of this is straightforward: if the sound is welcome or attractive it can greatly enhance the experience, but if not it may literally repel people. This is especially the case with music, which is not only a matter of personal taste, but can also strongly reflect our social group.

As a fan of classical music I was somewhat saddened to learn that the masterworks of the great composers are being piped into hotspots of anti-social behaviour to deter gangs from loitering. At Elm Park underground station, robberies dropped by 33 per cent and assaults on staff by 25 per cent within 18 months of the musical strategy being implemented[6] – a somewhat depressing, but potent example of how powerful people's tastes are in determining their behaviour. Ask yourself *'What kind of music appeals to our customers? How can we use music to enhance the customer experience?'*

Starbucks – coffee and music

Many shops choose the music they play carefully, as a way to build their credibility with customers. Starbucks have taken this further than most, by selling a range of eclectic artists that they feel match their customers' tastes. Writing for *Business Week*, Stanley Holmes concludes, 'Starbucks has never been primarily about the coffee. Its pell-mell growth ... has always been about selling an experience.'[7]

As with all the other senses, we use the sound a product makes to infer its qualities. Legendary ad man David Ogilvy used the absence of sound to emphasise the quality of Rolls-Royce cars back in the 1960s, using the line, 'At 60 miles an hour, the loudest noise in this new Rolls-Royce comes from the electric clock.'[8] By way of contrast, the loud crunch of a potato crisp is often considered as a good indicator of its freshness. Ask yourself *'How might we use sound to convey the qualities of our product?'*

To hear requires the least effort of any sense, and since technology is always progressing to reduce the burden of effort, it is no surprise that voice activated devices are slowly creeping from science fiction to reality. Audiobooks are already extremely popular, requiring less effort to ingest the contents than reading. When conveying information to the customer, ask yourself *'Might communicating using sound reduce the effort required on the part of the customer?'*

TASTE

There are very few social occasions which do not involve some kind of food or drink. Eating, drinking and socialising are all but inseparable: very few people like to eat at a restaurant alone. Food and drink are also commonly used to show appreciation. When invited to a friend's for dinner you might bring a bottle of wine, or offer to bring a dish.

Wiggle – an unexpected pleasure

I recently ordered some cycling kit from online retailer Wiggle. When I opened the packaging alongside my order were two small packets of Haribo sweets. It's often nice, unexpected touches like this that can make the experience that little bit better, and stop customers straying to the competition.

In the context of a customer experience then, food and drink can not only add a pleasurable social dimension, it can be used as a token of appreciation, or as a way to make customers feel welcome.

MULTI-SENSORY EXPERIENCES

Having given a brief summary of how each sense can be used to enhance the customer experience, I'd like to conclude this section with examples of how two very different businesses have succeeded by creating a compelling multi-sensory experience.

The Fat Duck – a multi-sensory experience like no other

What makes The Fat Duck such a special place is chef Heston Blumenthal's belief that eating is a truly multi-sensory experience. Often working with psychologists and scientists, his passionate curiosity has led him to craft a culinary experience where each sense has been considered with unparalleled rigour. Explaining his philosophy Heston says, 'Of course I want to create food that is delicious, but this depends on so much more than simply what's going on in the mouth – context, history, nostalgia, emotion, memory and the interplay of sight, smell, sound and taste all play an important part in our appreciation and enjoyment of food.'[9]

This approach has not only led to innovative dishes like the famous bacon and egg ice cream, but also to playing sounds to diners through headphones, and dispersing evocative aromas with dry ice. The results speak for themselves: crowned the best restaurant in the world in 2005 by *Restaurant Magazine*, and the best restaurant in the UK five years in a row by *The Good Food Guide*, The Fat Duck currently holds three Michelin stars. Heston himself has received honours as varied as an OBE from Her Majesty the Queen in 2006, and *GQ Magazine*'s Man of the Year in 2004, 2010 and 2011.[10] The message is quite clear: concentrate on delighting the senses and the world will beat a path to your door.

Toni&Guy – a multi-sensory experience

Hairdressers Toni&Guy have clearly worked hard to provide a great multi-sensory experience that extends beyond just getting your hair cut. Lying back to have my hair washed I quickly noticed the TV screens angled down from the ceiling that play music videos on their own channel *Toni&Guy TV*. After a head massage, you return to the chair where you are offered a choice of drinks to enjoy while you have your hair cut. The experience therefore includes sight, sound, touch and taste. It even includes smell if you opt to buy one of their many haircare products. It's obviously

▶

working: in 2011 Toni&Guy was voted as a SuperBrand for the fourth time. They now have over 420 salons across the world and employ over 7000 employees. In 2008 Toni Mascolo was awarded an honorary OBE.[11]

The rest of this chapter provides some general guidelines to consider when trying to improve the sensory experience:

Compensate for sensory deprivation

We seldom consider how critical our senses are until we find ourselves unable to use them. As we get older our senses may not be as keen as they once were, and many are affected by sensory disabilities. Don't sweep this problem under the carpet: there are great opportunities out there for those who can make their products and services accessible to everyone. You may even find that by making your products easier to use for those with a sensory impairment, you make it better for everyone else too. I have heard countless people praise the Kindle e-book reader because they can enlarge the text size to make it easier to read. Do not treat accessibility as an afterthought. Ask yourself *'How can we make this product or service work well for those with a sensory disability?'*

OXO GoodGrips – accessibility is good for business

The company OXO International was started by entrepreneur Sam Farber in 1989 to develop a range of easy-to-use kitchen utensils inspired by his wife's arthritis. The GoodGrips peeler, for example, had a thicker handle to make it easier to hold. They quickly found that tools designed to be usable by those with limited dexterity were also more comfortable and attractive to everyone else: OXO now sell over 850 products, they have won over 150 international design awards,[12] and grew sales at an average of 27 per cent from 1991 to 2009.[13]

It is not only disability that can deprive us of our senses: it happens whenever we go online. Our inability to touch, smell or taste an item when shopping on the web can hinder decision making, especially when buying tactile products like clothes or groceries. Surprisingly few have made progress in this area, I suspect because of the cost of compensatory measures, like close-up photography that reveals the texture of objects, or compelling verbal descriptions. I believe we will see great progress in this area over the coming years. Why not make fuller use of sound and video clips to compensate for a loss of touch? Marketers have successfully done this with television advertising for years. When faced with a situation where senses are ruled out, ask yourself *'How can we employ the other senses to compensate?'*

Offer a time-out

At times it is easy to feel like our senses are under assault. On the street music blares from shop fronts and leaks from headphones. Adverts on every surface compete for our attention. At the office many receive hundreds of e-mails, instant messages and phone calls a day, set against the background hum of machinery and chit chat. This not only ruins our ability to concentrate, it can leave us wanting time out.

The 'Naked Streets' of Drachten – psychological traffic calming

How do you decrease congestion while improving road safety? One approach that has been a great success in the Netherlands, and now in the UK, is to remove as many signs and signals as possible. This counter-intuitive approach works because instead of just following the signs, the ambiguity of the surroundings forces drivers to slow down and concentrate on what's going on around them, making eye contact with other drivers and looking out for pedestrians. The town of Drachten in the Netherlands, which first adopted this approach, has removed all its traffic lights despite having over 22,000 cars a day travelling through the town. They saw the number of accidents at one junction fall from 36 over

▶

four years to just two in the last two years. Similar results have been seen in Denmark and in the UK, where research showed a 35 per cent drop in accidents on roads where the centre-line was removed.[14] This is a fascinating example of how removing a stimulus from an environment can aid concentration and direct behaviour in a positive way.

In an environment where we are constantly over-stimulated, experiences that soothe are always welcome. It may be that less is actually more. By reducing the intensity of the experience, or eliminating some sensory intrusions, the experience might be greatly enhanced. Ask yourself *'Should we stimulate or soothe the sense? What could we eliminate from the environment to make it more relaxing?'*

The Beetle and Wedge – mobile tax

This peaceful restaurant by the river near where I live has a fun scheme to prevent the annoying intrusion of mobile phones: anyone who answers a phone is fined £5, anyone caught making a call at their table is fined £10. The money goes to charity.

Aim for consistency

Most companies I've worked with use a large number of different freelancers, design agencies and in-house teams, depending on the size, complexity and nature of the brief. The result is that the look and feel of their products and services can resemble a patchwork quilt. We even see pages of the same website having different stylistic treatments, which can lead to no end of confusion. A consistent look and feel across all products, services and media at every stage of the customer journey is important. It helps to make the brand recognisable, and reinforces the message you are trying to communicate.

Vivobarefoot – consistency across media

This brand of shoe is quite unlike most others on the market. Vivobarefoot believe that the best design for a shoe is one that allows our feet to move as if they were barefoot: allowing our toes to spread and our feet to feel the surface we are moving across. Doing so discourages a heel-striking running technique and so can reduce the likelihood of injury. To achieve this, the soles of the shoes are necessarily very thin, but must be tough and puncture proof too. Vivobarefoot are also proud of their ethical stance: the shoes are made using eco-friendly materials and production techniques.[15]

By printing their business cards on a material called Tyvek, which is not only tear-proof, but also incredibly thin, light and 100 per cent recyclable, they have managed to communicate all of the qualities of their product as well as their contact details. Most cards I get are filed away for safe keeping, but this one has managed to linger in my wallet for a while. I've shown it to quite a few people too.

Bookend the process with briefing and testing

In order to create a sensory experience that satisfies both the functional and aesthetic requirements across every stage of the experience, the briefing and testing phases are absolutely critical. To produce a result that is at once usable and attractive is a real skill and in most cases requires a professional designer. The clarity of the brief that the designer is given not only determines the quality of their work, it also directly affects the eventual cost: a woolly brief can cause costs to double simply through endless amends. Furthermore, without thorough testing we will not know if our goals have been met. In my experience, during the rush to bring something to market, the brief is sacrificed in the urgency to 'get on with it', and the testing is compromised in the urgency to launch. I implore you to consider these phases not as peripheral, but central to the process. Once your stuff is out in the world it's too late.

Summary

- Every product or service is fundamentally a sensual experience, so the way in which our senses are stimulated must always have an end in mind, and never be arbitrary or left to chance.

- Every sense should be considered: they all offer abundant opportunities to enhance the customer experience and differentiate a product or service from the competition.

- Experiences are *multi-sensory* in nature: the senses must not just be considered in isolation, they must work together, and special consideration is required when the use of our senses is restricted.

- Intensity is an important consideration: our senses are continually bombarded from the moment we wake. Opportunities lie in soothing as well as stimulating the senses.

- Consistency is key: a *common design language* should apply to every interaction to communicate the message unambiguously.

- The final design must be the result of carefully considered action: a thorough brief and rigorous testing are essential.

11

Great customer experiences are socially engaging

The importance of cultivating personal relationships with customers cannot be over-stated: we more readily buy from a friend than a stranger. However, our position within a social group is also a powerful and private motivator. Those experiences that elevate our status are often the most highly valued. This chapter will show you how to engage your customers on a social level.

Trade is a social act. J.S. MILL

Every now and then I am reminded just how basic the mechanics of business really are. It's easy to get sucked into the sham complexity of it all: the Gantt charts, gearing ratios, strategy decks, SWOTS, PESTS and the meaningless jargon. They're an easy way to blur the boundaries between activity and progress, or lend gravitas to the banal, but in doing so we also forget just how simple things can and should be.

As a case in point, my friend Ben called me a couple of years ago. He said he'd just got off the phone with a lovely woman who'd been really helpful sorting out his car insurance. He said I should give her a call; she might be able to sort me out too. I instantly forgot. A week later, he called me again to say he'd spoken to her again; she had a name now – Sarah Jayne – and again he said I should call her. He'd clearly made a new friend.

A week or so later, I did call her. It was immediately after yet another infuriating encounter with my then insurance provider. I'd spent for ever being passed around various departments, waiting on hold and talking to mandroids who could only tell me what their computers told them. True to Ben's word, she really was lovely: friendly, warm, polite and interested. For a moment I thought I'd entered a strange parallel universe: here I was, applying for insurance over the phone, not wanting to kill myself. I was actually enjoying it.

Let's fast forward to today: Ben has his car and household contents insured with her. I have both cars and my house contents insured with her. I have told everyone in the known universe (known to me that is) about how good she is to deal with. Last week I received a newsletter from her company telling me they are moving: they've grown to the extent that they need larger premises. Consider the context. In an industry dominated by huge players and price comparison sites, set against the backdrop of economic turmoil, a small town brokerage is doing a roaring trade, outgrowing its offices.

Here's another couple of names: Andrew Hill and Eilidh Ferguson. I met them through being a customer of theirs when they worked at a local café but now we're friends. Andy is a great chef, and Eilidh, who works front-of-house, is one of the most welcoming, accommodating hosts I've had the pleasure of being served by. They recently opened their own pub, an act of madness the media would assure you: pubs are closing at a rate of 50 a week![1] Well, they've only been open for a month or two, and getting a table for dinner already involves booking days in advance. They can't cope with the demand.

I could go on: Paul Lee owns a picture framing business in Oxford's Covered Market. He's a lovely guy, great at what he does, and has a genuine passion for his business that you can sense from the moment he opens his mouth. I've not bought a picture frame elsewhere for nine years, even though I have to wait a few weeks: he's always busy you see.

Is it mere coincidence that I know these people by name, that they are a genuine pleasure to be around, and that their businesses are a great success? I think not. If anything it's the *reason* for their success. Human beings are social creatures. It's in our DNA. There's a reason why solitary confinement is almost unbearable: we need social interaction to be healthy and happy. When it comes to a customer experience then, those that make doing business a social pleasure stand head and shoulders above the competition.

Make it personal

A warm welcome by attentive, charismatic staff stands out like a beautiful, handwritten letter in a sea of junk mail, and one moment of outstanding personal service can leave an indelible impression on a customer. I've collected great examples from friends over the years, probably my favourite is a friend's mother who is still raving about a bank clerk who paid a home visit when she was taken ill over 50 years ago.

Vitsoe Shelving – personal service
Date: Tue, 27 October 2009 at 7:25 PM

Hi Matt

It's been a little while but I wanted to send a note to ask how your installation had gone of your bay of shelves. I hope that they have been useful and that everything went well in putting them up. I remember you were installing it in your barn and it would be great to see a photo of your space if possible.

Get in touch if there is anything else I can help with.

Best wishes
Nick

There is much to be gained by adding a personal touch to the customer experience. Whether it's just remembering a customer's name, building a genuine friendship, or catering for an unusual request. In a world where we are often treated like digits and feel dwarfed by the size of the enterprise, to be treated as an individual is truly refreshing. This is easier than ever with social media services like Facebook and Twitter. Just today I booked my car in for a service simply by sending a Facebook message to the director of the garage I use. Ask yourself 'How can we add a personal touch to the experience?'

Japan Airlines – thank you notes

First class travellers on Japan Airlines often receive a handwritten thank you note from their cabin crew when disembarking. Some passengers have been known to collect them. Customers don't have to pay a huge premium to be treated like individuals, though. Opportunities are everywhere. Why not think about how you can offer a personal thank you to your customers. It's nice to feel appreciated.

A fantastic piece in the *New York Herald Tribune* quoted a Mr G.L. Clements of Jewel Stores Chicago, who has some thoughts on what makes a good customer experience:

> The supermarket that 'offers the shopper the subtle, psychological values' will have a better chance to build a profitable customer following than one which depends solely on low price and good quality merchandise ...

> In determining how to provide 'psychological values' attractive to the customer, Mr Clements said he thought a business should seek to develop 'the same traits that we like in our friends'. He outlined these traits as being cleanliness, up-to-date appearance, generosity, courtesy, honesty, patience, sincerity, sympathy and good-naturedness. Each store operator, he said, should ask himself whether the store has these traits ...[2]

That was on 10 May 1949 – over 60 years ago. If only his advice had been heeded. Nowadays if we even get to speak to someone there is a strong chance they will exhibit none of those qualities, often through no fault of their own. It is more than likely that their performance is assessed by the number of calls they are able to handle in a day. They will also be unable to express any sincerity or good-naturedness, since they will have an approved script to read from. By the time they get to you it's probably the hundredth time they've said the same thing that day. Unfortunately, there is a strong tendency for employees to treat the customer the way they are treated themselves by the organisation, and they aren't always treated well. Employees, especially those on the front line, are a hugely undervalued resource in every business I've worked with.

Clearly a waiter's job is so much more than carrying the food from the kitchen to the table. Likewise a call centre worker does much more than simply handling queries. The same goes for the guy stacking shelves in the supermarket. These people are the personification of the business: they are its human face. We don't often deal with the chef, the boss or the manager. With this in mind, in addition to their daily duties it's worth considering the vital roles that they can and should be playing.

Your employees are your USP

If you own a traditional bricks and mortar shop, what is stopping your customers from buying your product or service online, for a lower price at greater convenience? If the answer is 'nothing', you are probably already in trouble. Last year it was announced that the high street bookseller Waterstones would be closing 11 branches, US retailer Borders is also in dire-straits; and yet according to *The Guardian*, 'after years of falling sales and closures, many independents are now flourishing, marking themselves out from the high-discount competition by offering character, wide-ranging live events and personal service'. The new managing director at Waterstones is now doing his best to 'return to the chain's traditional values of individuality and highly knowledgeable service'.[3]

If I just wanted to buy a book I could simply go online and do it. But I also like to browse, and discover something new. I like it when people recommend something to me. Knowledgeable, passionate staff can add a personal touch to the customer experience that a website simply can't match. Ask yourself '*What do our staff bring to the experience that cannot be easily imitated by competitors? How can their knowledge, passion and skill make for a unique experience?*'

Trailfinders – knowledgeable, friendly staff

At the time of writing, travel agents are closing down left, right and centre. Household name Thomas Cook reported a £398 million loss in 2011 and is now closing 200 branches in a bid to turn things around.[4] The cause of their demise is not just the economic downturn, it's the rise of online booking and price comparison sites like travelsupermarket.com, lastminute.com or kayak.co.uk.

How then is Trailfinders flourishing? The answer: expert staff and great personal service. Online reviews praise their staff, who seem to have spent their lives travelling, and so can piece together an ideal itinerary for almost any trip. As a nice touch, when you log in to see your itinerary online there is a photo in the top-right corner of the person who took your booking, along with their contact details, which does a lot to humanise the business.

The results speak for themselves: in 2012 Trailfinders topped the *Which? Consumer Travel Survey*, scoring 97 per cent customer satisfaction. They also won the *Which? Best Travel Company* award in 2011 among other plaudits from the *Daily Telegraph*, *The Guardian* and *The Sunday Times*.[5] How did I hear about them? A friend referred me of course.

Everyone works in marketing

Not so long ago I was returning home from London on the train and ended up chatting with the man sitting opposite me. Conversation turned to our professional lives, and he explained that he worked in waste management. I said I'd always wondered what happened after the recycling had been collected, and to my surprise we spent the next half-hour engrossed in conversation about it. He explained to me how advanced their facilities were, that they were able to sort through the rubbish automatically using lasers that could tell different materials apart. To my surprise I found our conversation quite fascinating. He spoke with genuine passion for his work, not something you'd expect when talking about rubbish. Mike (I remember his name) did a better job of promoting the company he worked for than any advert could.

Every employee works in marketing: they could be telling friends and family what a great business they work for, about the cool products and services they offer. Better yet, they could actually be showing people. They are in a uniquely trusted position to share their opinion with credibility and confidence. Ask yourself *'What message are our staff communicating about our business? How can we make them our most trusted advocates?'*

Your people are your loyalty scheme

It is far easier to be loyal to a person than to a brand: we place more trust in those we have a personal relationship with, and more readily buy from a friend than a stranger. Would you rather get your morning coffee from the shop where they greet you as a friend and know your order before you ask, or the one where they don't even say hello? It is unlikely that my friend Ben and I will buy insurance from anyone but SJ even if it's cheaper. Likewise with my business bank. I know the manager and have done for years. When I need something I can just call, text or e-mail them and it's taken care of.

Your front-line staff are your research team

On most of the projects I work on there is a requirement for research. We need to get a feel for the territory and get to know as much as possible about customers and the movements of the market. The usual approach is to hire a research consultancy to come in, take a brief, then disappear to report back in a month or two. Most clients also conduct workshops where customers come into the office and voice their opinions.

This has always struck me as a bit odd. Surely we have people who are dealing with customers every day in shops, call centres, or out on the road? Better still, why aren't management spending time on the shopfloor themselves to develop a rich feel for what's really going on?

Why aren't software developers working an hour or two a week on the helpdesk so that they understand their customers' frustrations?

In the last seven years I have seen a senior manager perform a customer-facing role zero times. Before paying for research why not make the most of what you've got? Get down on the shopfloor and ask your staff: they'll appreciate feeling involved in making improvements. Better still, walk a mile in their shoes and see for yourself. Ask yourself *'Are the front-line staff contributing meaningfully to improving our customer experience?'*

Your people are your contingency plan

You can tell a lot about a business by how things are handled when they go wrong. In fact, we often rate a customer experience more highly if we experience a problem that is well resolved than if we never experienced one at all. All too often when something goes awry, the emphasis is solely on getting us back to the position we'd be in if we'd never had the problem in the first place. This approach ignores the costs associated with the problem: the wasted time, effort, and loss of enjoyment.

Ritz-Carlton – $2000 per guest

Every staff member of the Ritz-Carlton hotel chain is authorised to spend up to $2000 on a guest, per incident(!), to create a wonderful experience for the customer. Critically this is not just in the case of a problem, it's if an opportunity presents itself to do something outstanding. One example includes building a wooden walk-way down to the beach with a tent set up for a man and his wife (who was in a wheelchair) to have dinner,[6] not as a customer request, but off their own backs. This attitude is clearly ingrained in the Ritz-Carlton culture, and training is a major factor in turning this into a reality. But any business could give its front-line staff a set of customer experience guidelines to follow as part of their training. This would not only make their jobs more rewarding by giving them a little more autonomy, but would also tune them into noticing opportunities and issues. Everybody wins.

You can reap enormous benefits by treating problems as opportunities to show flair, commitment and caring, rather than waiting to be bullied into compensation by your customer, or doing the bare minimum to get them back on the rails where they came off. Ask yourself *'How can we turn a negative into a positive? When mistakes happen how can we show that we really care?'*

When disputes arise, it's all too easy to focus on who's right or wrong: if the customer is at fault, why should you do anything? Put your sword down for a second, and ask yourself 'What's more important, being right or being liked? What's really in your interests: feeling smug or building a long-term relationship? There is also one more crucial thing to bear in mind: the word 'customer' means a lot more than just who pays the bill. When we become a customer, we automatically become endowed with a privileged status. In our minds, to be a customer is to be important. From this point on the business is there to serve us, and to serve is to be a servant. This is worth reflecting on for a minute.

Status update

Think about a bad customer experience that you've had. Maybe a waiter was rude to you, or someone didn't return your call. Perhaps you called up to ask for assistance and they refused to help you. Maybe you went into a shop, and rather than offer to help, the staff just stood around chatting among themselves. All of these experiences are unpleasant to us because they diminish our status: it is a failure to recognise our importance, to honour and respect our higher standing that is the root of the problem.

This privileged status is universal: it is a fundamental part of being a customer. It applies whether we are buying a doughnut or a Bentley. When a business acts like they don't care about us, it's a status issue. In a customer's head, other customers do not exist, or if they do, they aren't as important as we are. One of the worst possible things you can say to a customer is, 'I've got a hundred other customers I need to deal with today. You are taking up too much time.' It makes us feel insignificant.

The subject of status often goes unconsidered because it is an intensely personal and private issue. To mention it is almost taboo, or at least considered ill-mannered, but just because it goes unsaid does not make it unimportant. As Alain De Botton's book *Status Anxiety* explains, '… high status is thought by many (but freely admitted by few) to be one of the finest of earthly goods… We all suffer – to a greater or lesser degree, usually privately and with embarrassment – from status anxiety.'[7] We care, even if we don't share.

Bloomberg Software – an unusual status symbol

The pleasure derived from status can account for all manner of bizarre behaviours. I came across a fascinating example of this recently, when reading an article about Bloomberg's financial markets software. The design of the user interface is generally accepted as hideous, complex and difficult to use, yet resistance to a re-design from the users is strong. Why? Its mastery is seen as a status symbol.

As Dominique Leca writes in *UX Magazine*, 'The pain inflicted by blatant UI (user interface) flaws is strangely transformed into the rewarding experience of looking like a hard-core professional. The Bloomberg Terminal interface looks terrible, but it allows traders to pretend that you need to be experienced and knowledgeable to use it. Users favour complexity and clutter over efficiency and clarity to sustain a fictive status symbol.'[8]

Status is not just about conspicuous displays of wealth, or trying to impress our neighbours, it's much broader than that. Nobody enters the Olympics with their heart set on coming in seventh: they want to be number one, gold. You might dream of being the boss one day; you probably don't dream of being someone's minion. Status is fundamentally important to all of us. We crave it, not least of all because it's good for us. In *The Pursuit of Pleasure*, Lionel Tiger explains how experiments show that elevated status actually changes our brain and body chemistry, increasing levels of a secretion called serotonin, which has been shown to play a variety of roles in our health and well-being.

Tiger concludes, 'The central fact is that a substance that the body generates is stimulated by an individual's social position. When the substance reaches a certain level, the individual exhibits characteristics of comfort and good health … He or she enjoys better physical, and presumably, mental health than individuals lower in the hierarchical system … Status differences translate into physiological ones. Both lower status and uncertainty about status are physiologically disturbing. They are also likely to be psychologically disquieting.'[9] In other words high status is not only pleasurable, it's good for our health.

Bugaboo Donkey – the £1200 pushchair

It seems there is no object that cannot be used to confer status on its owner. Witness the Bugaboo Donkey – the first baby stroller to break the thousand-pound barrier. Who would pay that amount for something the baby will literally grow out of in a relatively short time? Actually, a lot of people. When the Donkey was released in 2011 eager parents had to be placed on a waiting list. A spokesman from high street retailer John Lewis said, 'It's been massive. We've been selling the equivalent of one an hour over the last week which is very impressive given that it's such an expensive product.'[10]

The implications for customer experiences are clear: the experiences that we enjoy the most are those that elevate our status and make us feel important. For each stage of the customer journey ask yourself the simple question *'What are we doing to make the customer feel important?'*

Summary

- Human beings are social creatures. Those that make doing business a social pleasure stand head and shoulders above the competition.

- One moment of outstanding personal service can leave an indelible impression on a customer.

- Where possible add a personal touch to the customer experience.

- Front-line staff are the human embodiment of the business: they are a precious asset.

- Your employees are potentially a powerful source of differentiation – put their knowledge and personalities to good use.

- Remember that every employee works in marketing. What are they saying about your business?

- It is far easier to be loyal to a person than to a brand. Building personal relationships with customers will keep them coming back.

- Your front-line staff know more about your customers than anyone else. Put their expertise to use to improve your customer experience. You are already paying for them, and they'll feel more valued too – everybody wins.

- Treat problems as opportunities to show flair, commitment and caring. Don't just do the bare minimum.

- When we become a customer, we automatically become endowed with a privileged status. Above all else, make every customer feel important.

Great customer experiences put the customer in control

Control is fundamentally important to us: we want to do things in our own time and in our own way, and we take exception to those encounters that force us to jump through hoops. By contrast, we appreciate experiences that are flexible, accommodating and leave us feeling in control. This chapter explores how we can maximise the customer's feeling of control most effectively, without overloading them with choice.

I did it my way. FRANK SINATRA

We don't just want to achieve our goals, we also want to achieve them *our way*. There is a sound psychological reason for this. The influential Self-Determination Theory developed by psychologists Edward Deci and Richard Ryan is one of many that emphasises the importance of feeling in control to our well-being. Their theory states that we have three innate psychological needs: *relatedness* – the need to socialise and connect with others; *competence* – a feeling that we are in control of our environment; and *autonomy* – the exercise of our free will.[1] We all want to feel like we are the masters of our own destiny.

The urge to control can be so strong that many spend more time and energy at work trying to gain control of projects than they do making those projects a success. Anyone who has worked in a large corporation will tell you that people rarely surrender control of something voluntarily, and many are not especially keen on surrendering control to the customer either. When it comes to customer experiences, control is often most noticeable by its absence. We've all felt that sinking feeling of not quite being sure who's boss: maybe we want to discuss a problem with someone but won't be put through; maybe we don't have enough expertise to know whether we're being ripped off. We might find we have signed a contract for a service that doesn't live up to expectations but must now wait for it to expire before we can move onto something better. In these situations we find ourselves almost at the mercy of the business we are spending money with. It's not a great feeling.

Fortunately, technological advances have empowered the consumer in ways that were unimaginable a couple of decades ago. This has not gone unnoticed and many businesses are having to make significant changes to the way they operate. Vodafone Group CEO, Vittorio Colao, is one of many who have found themselves faced with this new reality: 'It is not the brand talking any more and telling the customer what to do ... it is the customer who will decide, I am trying to steer the whole company in this direction.'[2] To create the best possible experience then, we need to make sure the customer feels in control every step of the way.

Freedom of choice

To give the customer more control, the most common approach is simply to offer more choice over *where* and *when* they interact with the business, and *what* they buy. This may provide more control in the literal sense, since the customer has greater decision-making power, but this approach has its downsides. Offering more choice only gives the customer more control up to a point. As we saw in the chapters on stress and effort, the greater the choice, the harder it is to decide. Beyond a point, offering more choice actually makes the customer feel less in control.

Neither does transferring more decision-making power to the customer necessarily result in them having more control. Most people I know who have digital SLR cameras never take them off the automatic mode: if forced to decide the settings manually, they wouldn't be able to set the exposure correctly to take a nice picture. They may have decision-making power but they don't really have control over the end result.

Control must be proportional to skill, so competence is a key factor in deciding how much direct control is desirable to the customer. In many situations we recognise that others are best placed to make decisions for us, and so to gain control over successfully achieving our objectives, we surrender some control over the minutiae. This usually also has the welcome effect of reducing the burden of effort. I don't want to spend my weekends fussing over my accounts – I want to delegate that, and in doing so I surrender control of the task, but gain control of my time. Unfortunately, one type of control tends to offset another.

Switching perspectives, the more choice we offer the customer, the more expensive it gets for the business. The more products we create, the more channels we operate in, and the more hours we are open, the greater the cost. If, for example, we decide to develop a suite of mobile and tablet apps, kiosks and social media offerings to go alongside our shop, website or call centre, we run the risk of spreading our resources too thin. I've seen plenty of businesses do exactly this with no rationale for these projects beyond simply offering more choice to the customer. They start off by saying, 'We want to do a mobile app', then figure out what it will do later. Choosing between three different channel options all of which are poorly conceived and executed is of no benefit to anyone: the customer won't use it, and the money may as well have been tossed on a fire.

To create a decent customer experience that works seamlessly across multiple touchpoints can be a massive undertaking. The more touchpoints you add and the more functionality you want to support, the more complex it gets. Some companies are having to redo their whole technology infrastructure in order to try to achieve this kind of seamless experience, at vast expense and, from what I've seen, with limited success.

In stark contrast to the omni-channel, 24/7/365, infinite-choice mentality that many businesses have embraced, I believe that we should strive to offer customers *appropriate* choices, rather than simply the maximum possible. We shouldn't just throw mud at the wall in the hope that some will stick: choice for choice's sake is detrimental to both the customer experience and the profitability of the business. The real challenge is to establish how much choice is enough, and what it is exactly that we should allow the customer to choose. Rather than offering a prescriptive solution to this challenge, I will instead look at those elements of the experience that customers commonly seek control over and explain why this is, by relating these factors back to the principles we have covered so far.

There are two benefits to this approach: first, it will allow you to give customers control where it is most effective in improving the experience; second, it will allow you to prioritise your efforts and make the most effective use of your budget. This will also provide a useful recap of many of the principles we've covered so far, and offer a glimpse of how they work together in practice. To get started, here are the things that customers most commonly want to control.

Control over when

Time is our most precious resource. The internet revolutionised the way we do business because it allowed us to perform many kinds of transaction when it suited us best. It suited most companies too: servers are cheaper than people and buildings.

Controlling when we do things isn't about choice per se, it's about minimising the effort required to complete a task by making it more convenient. As such I find it more useful to focus the discussion on convenience rather than choice, since it keeps the specific needs of the customer in mind: we could keep our call centre or shop open 24 hours a day which gives the ultimate in choice, but it may not be worth it if there is little demand outside certain periods. It may be that convenience can be increased by making more staff available at peak hours to reduce wait times, conversely it may be that staying open late so people can shop after work makes all the difference, especially if competitors have shut at 5 p.m. on the dot. Ask yourself *'Can we make the product or service more convenient for the customer by changing when they can use it?'*

Giving customers control over their time is not just about giving them choice over when they do things, it's about managing their expectations about when things will happen – anything uncertain is inherently out of our control. Waiting around all day for a courier or service engineer to arrive is frustrating. Furthermore, we often don't know how long a task will take to complete, so we can't plan our time effectively. Ask yourself *'How can we set better expectations about when things will happen? Can we let customers know how long a task will take?'*

Ocado – control over your time

Award-winning online supermarket Ocado allow you to specify when you want your shopping delivered by choosing an hour-long time slot between 6 a.m. and 11:30 p.m.

There are two principles at work here that give the customer a feeling of control: Ocado are reducing the effort required from the customer by making their offering as convenient as possible, and they are setting accurate expectations that remove uncertainty from the experience.

Control over where

The promise of multi-channel customer experiences has been to give the customer more control over where they interact with us: they can order online and collect from the store, or shop in-store and have it delivered to their home. They can follow their favourite brands on social media, and access many services from a smart-phone. Again, much like giving the customer control over when things happen, this isn't really about choice, it's about convenience – reducing the amount of effort required from the customer.

This is where I think the omni-channel advocates have got it wrong. Many people believe that the Holy Grail of customer experiences is to offer everything through every touchpoint. I disagree: to do so is hugely expensive, and different touchpoints have different capabilities and are better suited to different tasks. A smart-phone, for example, is not ideally suited for entering large volumes of data: for those kinds of tasks a device with a larger keyboard and screen is still preferable.

Before extending a service to a new touchpoint, ask yourself *'Why would the customer want to do this on this touchpoint? What is unique about the touchpoint that we can take advantage of? Is it genuinely more convenient, or are we just doing it to offer more choice?'*

UK Train Times – control through convenience

This mobile app is a great example of using a touchpoint to its strengths in service of a genuine customer need. The app allows you to check train times between two destinations, which is useful, but also lets you set your local station which allows two neat features. The first is that you can check the local departure list including tracking the progress of trains along the line, so if a train is late you know by how much. The second is that by using the GPS function of the phone you can just press 'Next train home' and it will figure out your nearest station and the next available train. Both are ways of reducing the effort required from the customer.

Control over what we spend

One area where businesses have been reluctant to offer their customers more control is when it comes to their spending. Quotes can have a nasty habit of escalating, and hidden charges, complex and confusing pricing models and poor communication can combine to rob us of control. This may earn the business a quick buck in the short term, but it creates a simmering resentment among customers. Given half the chance they will go elsewhere, and certainly won't be singing your praises.

Ultimately, offering customers greater control over their spending is just another form of expectation management. If your competitors are sneaking a profit by robbing the customer of control over their spending, they are opening the door for you to compete on honesty, transparency and simplicity. Ask yourself *'How can we offer the customer more control over their spending?'*

Vodafone Data Test Drive – control your spending

Choosing the right data plan for a smart-phone can be problematic. Most people – myself included – really have no idea what a gigabyte looks like in terms of e-mails, videos or downloads: it's just an arbitrary number. The result is that many smart-phone users have received unexpectedly huge bills. Vodafone have started to make some progress in this area, offering a service called Data Test Drive. For the first three months of your contract you can use unlimited data on your phone with no additional charge for exceeding the amount on your bundle. At the end of this period you are shown how your consumption compares to your allowance, and offered the option to change it if there is a discrepancy. You can also track your usage through an app on the phone or your account on their website. This helps you get a feel for your usage and prevents the shock of a huge bill at the end of your first month.

Control over who we spend it with

At the most basic level we want to control who we do business with – we want to decide whether we stay on as a customer or take our business elsewhere. Unfortunately we often find ourselves locked into contracts that give us little room to manoeuvre, and can end up feeling beholden to the company, rather than the other way around. The longer the term of the contract, the more of a commitment it is, and so the more time and effort must be put into making the decision. These kinds of agreements can put customers off. Some companies have made this easier by allowing the customer to try before they buy through free trial periods; others have gone a step further, eliminating almost any on-going commitment at all.

There is a big difference between staying on as a customer because you are satisfied, and staying because you have to, and it shows far greater confidence in your offering if you give customers the freedom to walk away. If all your competitors are locking their customers in, why not stand out from the crowd, and give them the freedom to choose? Get the rest of the experience right and they'll stay with you voluntarily and appreciate the goodwill on your part. Ask yourself *'Can we let customers try before they buy? Should we give customers more freedom to come and go?'*

Basecamp – manageable commitment and transparent pricing

37 Signals, the creators of project management and collaboration software Basecamp, have done a great job of putting the customer in control. When you visit the product information page on their website, there is a clear link to pricing options right at the top – they haven't buried it somewhere out of sight. When you visit this page the headline reads 'Honest prices, no surprises. Pay as you go. No long-term contracts. No per-user fees. You can switch packages or cancel at any time.' It lists four clear and simple pricing options, then at the bottom of the table, 'Get started today with a 45-day free trial. No obligation, no credit-card required.'[3]

Not only does this set accurate expectations about what your bill will be, giving you total control over your spending; it also gives you total control over whether you choose to remain a customer at all – another box ticked. Their openness and honesty makes you feel like this is a brand you can trust. They must be doing something right: at the time of writing, Basecamp are used to manage 8 million projects, in 180 countries in over 150,000 companies.[4]

It's not just choosing who we do business with that matters; we often want to choose who we deal with at that business. As we saw when looking at the social dimension of the customer experience, building personal relationships not only builds loyalty, it builds trust too. When we trust somebody we feel far more comfortable relinquishing control to them. Being able to specify who we deal with can also reduce the effort required to complete a task. It can be very frustrating explaining the details of a problem to five different people when what we really want to do is talk to the first person we dealt with. Ask yourself *'How can we give customers more control over who they deal with?'*

Accommodating unique customer requests is another opportunity to show that you care and add a personal touch to the experience. It may be as simple as taking an ingredient out of a meal, or posting something to their work address rather than their home, or working out of office hours to help meet a deadline. Either way, in a world where we must often jump through hoops to do things in the way that best suits the company, those experiences that offer a bit of flexibility are much appreciated.

Control over what things look like

Mass customisation and personalisation have been a reality for many years now, giving us unprecedented control over the appearance of things: we can customise everything from Zippo lighters to Nike trainers, and are shown personal recommendations when we shop online. Customisation and personalisation are hugely popular because they increase our control over how accurately our identity is reflected: it allows us to express our individuality. The challenge is to strike the balance in such a way that the choice is not overwhelming – the greater the choice, the more must be done to make that choice manageable.

Control over what things do

Every product or service we buy is in the service of an objective. The closer an offering is to matching our exact requirements, the more likely it is that we will choose it. Unfortunately, our requirements, even within a relatively narrow field, can be very diverse. The result has been an over-abundance of choice as product ranges have swelled to accommodate our every whim. The net result is usually less control rather than more since we often lack the competence to know which best fits our needs. I don't encounter many businesses that wouldn't be better off by cutting the number of products they offer.

This is especially the case when buying complex technology products. Friends often ask me for advice about which digital camera they should buy. They've tried their best to understand the options but don't feel confident to make a choice themselves: they don't feel in control. They always sound a bit crestfallen when I say I can't help them – I don't have a clue either. The same is true with almost every kind of technology product. When looking at the range of products you offer try to answer these questions:

1 Does each product or service solve a specific problem that the others in the range don't?

2 Are offerings differentiated along clear dimensions that the customer understands?

3 Are the differences between each product or service in your range self-evident?

4 Does the naming of each offering help clarify its position in the range?

5 Is the design of each product or service modular?

DOES EACH PRODUCT OR SERVICE SOLVE A SPECIFIC PROBLEM THAT THE OTHERS IN THE RANGE DON'T?

This is fundamental. When a new requirement comes up, don't release a whole new product if there isn't enough of a difference to justify it. Just improve the ones you've got.

Yvon Chouinard, founder and owner of outdoor clothing company Patagonia, makes the point nicely when outlining his product design philosophy: 'Designing for the foundation of filling a functional need focuses the design process and ultimately makes for a superior finished product. Without a serious functional demand we can end up with a product that, although it may look great, is difficult to rationalise as being in our line – i.e., "Who needs it?" ... Make fewer styles; design better.'[5]

ARE OFFERINGS DIFFERENTIATED ALONG CLEAR DIMENSIONS THAT THE CUSTOMER UNDERSTANDS?

On a functional level most products within a range differ along simple dimensions: size, weight, megapixels or horsepower for example. By organising the range along these dimensions, it becomes easier for the customer to choose which product is right for them. Furthermore, by allowing them to work through one parameter at a time, the process of choosing becomes far more manageable.

ARE THE DIFFERENCES BETWEEN EACH PRODUCT OR SERVICE IN YOUR RANGE SELF-EVIDENT?

Here are the descriptions for two Sony Vaio laptops on their web page entitled, 'Discover the VAIO Laptops range': C series – 'Colourful style and everyday essentials for work and play', E series – 'Stand out style and every day essentials for work and play'.[6] If we can't easily tell the difference between one product and another, we will likely choose neither.

DOES THE NAMING OF EACH OFFERING HELP CLARIFY ITS POSITION IN THE RANGE?

Here's a quick question for you: which of these Sony Vaio's is a desktop computer and which is a laptop: the L series, or the T series? Which is the thinnest of their laptops: the Z series or the S series? On their website the order actually goes: T, C, Z, S, E, J, L.[7] Obviously they aren't ordered alpha-numerically, but they aren't ordered by price, size or weight either. When I stepped through to look at the C series laptop the product name changed to VPCCB3P1E.[8] Choosing a product is far easier when we can see how it fits into the range. It also helps if the product name makes its function self-evident!

IS THE DESIGN OF EACH PRODUCT OR SERVICE MODULAR?

There is a lot to be said for making products or services in small modules that can fit together like Lego bricks: it's a situation where both the business and the customer usually win. Modular products allow us to upgrade individual parts without replacing the whole, and if one part fails we can repair it rather than throw the whole thing away as we have to do with many modern electronic products. It also allows the customer to configure products to their specific requirements, and from a business perspective it makes product development simpler too since these components can often be worked on in isolation.

Control is a resultant force

Imagine a ball on a table that has several forces working on it, each of different strengths and directions. The direction the ball will move in is determined by how all those forces add up into a *resultant force*. The overall amount of control the customer feels is like this resultant force, and each dimension of control we've covered – the who's, what's, when's and where's – contributes towards it. Sometimes these work in harmony, sometimes they work in opposition.

We might give customers complete control over their spending by offering a fixed monthly charge. This sets clear expectations that the bill will be the same every month, and has the added benefit of requiring less effort to understand; yet to make this profitable, it requires that the customer operates within fixed parameters of usage: in gaining control over their spending, they have diminished control over what they can use the service for. We may decide to give the customer more control over how the product reflects their identity by increasing the number of colour options available, but if we keep increasing the number of choices, stress factors start to work in opposition, and the overall sense of control is reduced.

Successfully increasing customer control is not as simple as just increasing choice; it requires striking the perfect balance between competing requirements. We must prioritise carefully: we cannot hope to pursue all available options at once without either exceeding the available time and budget, or compromising on quality.

Build-A-Bear

One example of a business which has managed to get this balance just right is toy retailer Build-A-Bear. You can go into their shop and build your own stuffed toy, either for yourself or, as when I went there, as a present for somebody. When I arrived at the store at first I felt a little overwhelmed: it was much busier than I expected, with lots of kids running around being entertained by the staff, who clearly knew how to make it the most fun experience possible. There seemed to be so much choice I wasn't quite sure where to start, but almost straight away an assistant came over to help me. He asked what kind of thing I was after, and told me about what was available with real enthusiasm, saying he would help me with it all the way through until it was finished. I explained to him that I'd popped out on a lunchbreak and wouldn't have much time, but he said not to worry, and that it shouldn't take longer than 20 minutes or so.

The process of building the bear is actually very organised and structured so that the choice isn't too overwhelming when you get started. There are several stations that you pass through to end up with the completed product. First you choose the basic character that you want at the *Choose Me* station.

Next you move onto the *Hear Me* station, where you can choose a sound module to put into the bear. To make this easy you can choose pre-recorded sounds, or you can even record your own ten-second message that will play. I opted to record my own message and the assistant showed me to a quiet spot at the back of the store where I could record it.

After that was done, we moved onto the *Stuff Me* stage. Here there is what looks like a giant candy-floss machine that whirls the stuffing around in a big drum where you can see it, with a pipe at the end where the stuffing comes out. The girl manning this stage asked me how firm I wanted the bear to be, and I opted to make my bear quite full so he could stand up himself. A nice touch at this stage is that although they need to stuff the bear themselves to make sure the stuffing is distributed correctly in the bear, there is a big pedal on the floor that controls the flow of the stuffing. They get you to press it on and off, so even though you aren't doing it yourself you still feel a part of it. Although for adults it's a bit cheesy, they also insist that you put in a little satin heart that brings the bear to life.

Before they sew the bear up for you – another thing they need to do themselves – they put in a unique barcode, so if the bear is ever lost it can be reunited with its owner. This is fantastic attention to detail: children can get very attached to their toys and this shows great empathy for the customer. With the bear almost finished, I chose some accessories – there is a great range of different outfits and extras to choose from. Then finally, I was shown to a computer where I could give the bear a name and print off their own personal birth certificate.

I actually really enjoyed the experience: the staff were great, the end result was exactly what I wanted, and most of all it was good fun. It's no surprise the shop was full, and parents and children alike all had smiles on their faces.

What makes the Build-A-Bear experience so exceptional is that they have got the balance between often opposing forces just right, to really make you feel in control of the finished result. The range of options was staggering but a well-structured store layout and friendly, helpful staff made it fun and easy. The clear pricing at each stage made it easy to keep a total of how much my furry friend was going to cost. They also make sure that they do the bits that require skill, like sewing up the bear at the end with the needle and thread, but do so in such a way that you feel that it is still *you* who is making the bear. I know quite a few people who have taken their children there and they've all come away impressed and entertained. We are not alone: since the business started in 1997 they have sold over 70 million bears and have over 400 stores across the world.[9] Clearly their staff think it's fun too. In 2012 they appeared on *Fortune*'s '100 best companies to work for' list for the fourth year in a row.[10]

Summary

- Customers don't just want to achieve goals, they also want to achieve them in their own way.

- To create the best possible experience we need to make sure the customer feels in control at every step of the journey.

- More choice and more decision-making power does not necessarily result in a greater feeling of control.

- Different types of control can offset each other: we may gain control of our time by delegating control of a task to somebody else.

- The more choice we offer, the more expensive it becomes for the business.

- We should aim to give customers control where it is most effective in improving the experience, in ways that make the most effective use of budget.

- Customers want control over *when* and *where* they perform a task, *how much* they spend and *who with*.

- When it comes to products we want to fine tune what the product looks like and what functions it performs to best reflect our identity and objectives.

- Each dimension of control – the who's, what's, when's and where's – contributes towards the overall feeling of control. Sometimes these work in harmony, sometimes they work in opposition.

- Successfully increasing customer control is not as simple as just increasing choice; it requires striking the perfect balance between competing requirements.

13

Great customer experiences consider the emotions

We are all slaves to our emotions, yet most see their customers from a purely rational perspective. In this chapter we will explore how evaluating the emotional aspect of an experience can bring often unconsidered issues to the surface and open up new ways to delight the customer.

Let's not forget, that the little emotions are the great captains of our lives and we obey them without realising it. VINCENT VAN GOGH

Introduction

When I was a kid, Sony was the definition of cool. The yellow sports Walkman was an 80s icon, and as time and technology marched on I marvelled at their new feather-touch machines, barely larger than the cassettes they played. When CDs became the dominant format it was a Sony Discman for me; I even had a MiniDisc player. To hold a Sony product in my hand felt as though I was holding a piece of the future, and I developed a fondness for Sony that few brands have matched since. Unfortunately, when I pick up a Sony product now, I feel like I am holding a piece of the past. I own a relatively new Sony TV and while the picture quality is fine the rest seems only average to me. Sony, which once stood out from the crowd because of their quality, design language and innovation, are now almost indistinguishable from most rivals.

I am saddened by the state of this once great company. According to the BBC, it has been seven years since their television unit has turned a profit.[1] In April 2012 they announced their biggest loss in history (around £3.5 billion).[2] There will be around 10,000 job losses.[3] What went wrong? To answer the question fully would take a book in itself, but I think it can be summed up in a single sentence: they lost their emotional appeal. Their televisions still work, their cameras take good photos, and their laptops are alright too, but that's the problem: nobody falls in love with something that's only average. We want something that plucks our heart-strings. The way a product, brand or service makes us *feel* is critical to its success.

These feelings play a central role at all stages of the customer life cycle. In the beginning we want a customer to choose our offering over a competitor; so it is critical that the first impression creates the right feeling. We also want the product or service to create positive feelings when in use: it is not enough to have a dazzling marketing campaign that gives us the warm fuzzies, the product must perform brilliantly too. Finally we want people to develop an 'emotional attachment' to the brand so that they continue to buy from us in the future and share their positive experiences with others.

To make this happen we must consider the specific emotions that we want to evoke during each stage of the customer experience. We must also accept from the outset that emotional appeal is not a substitute for functional brilliance: it's not the head or the heart, it's both. Many businesses fail because they create a beautifully evocative advert but a product that doesn't deliver the goods. This has the opposite effect of creating one of the most powerful negative emotions: disappointment.

There are three reasons why considering the emotional reaction of the customer is important:

1   Emotions can have specific 'action tendencies', so to encourage (or discourage) a specific behaviour we may need to evoke (or avoid) specific emotions.
2   Having a target emotional state for each stage of the customer experience provides a goal to work towards that brings empathy and focus to the design process.

3   Since emotions are often readily observable we can incorporate them into testing to validate our work, or identify opportunities for improvement.

Emotion action tendencies

Different emotions can result in different action tendencies,[4] so by actively avoiding or promoting specific feeling states we can encourage certain behaviours. When we experience anger – the feeling that typically occurs when our progress towards an objective is hampered – our tendency is to put more effort towards achieving the goal. Rather than giving up, getting angry makes us try harder.[5] This has interesting implications for the customer experience: annoyance and disappointment may cause us to complain, but it's anger that pushes us towards legal action or negative comments on social media.

Anxiety is another emotion with a strong action tendency: it makes us stop what we are doing, and become more wary of our surroundings.[6] This too can have a big impact on the customer experience, especially when buying online. If there is uncertainty about security during a check-out process, or we are not quite sure the product is the right one, we can abandon the sale at the last minute. This is why online retailers do their best to eliminate sources of stress during the check-out process: all possible distractions are removed, clear feedback is given during each step of the process, and retailers do their best to produce an interface that looks reassuringly professional and trustworthy.

Photojojo – interest = exploration

The product detail page of online photography accessories store Photojojo has an unusual feature. Next to the large image of the product is a picture of a lever, with the text 'DO NOT PULL' underneath. Obviously the first thing you do when you see that is press it, at which point an animated hand comes down from the top of the screen, grabs the page and pulls it up, showing the details of the product that were hidden below the page fold. This

▶

is a great example of how evoking a specific emotion (interest) encourages certain behaviours (exploration). This also injects some fun into the shopping experience.

Don't leave these action tendencies to chance. Ask yourself *'What actions do we want the user to take? What emotions would discourage or encourage these actions? How can these be promoted or avoided?'*

Define emotional success criteria

In this book so far I've written exclusively about how to break the customer experience down into its most simple elements. One criticism of a reductionist approach like this is that often the whole does not equal the sum of the parts. We might fuss over every detail but end up with a collection of details rather than an organic, cohesive whole. We might not be able to put our finger on exactly what is missing, but sometimes a product just doesn't *feel* right.

McLaren – too 'clinical'

As their website proudly states, 'McLaren Automotive has a singular vision: to produce the greatest supercars in the world. A team of passionate and obsessive enthusiasts, from our global network of retailers to our engineers in the new McLaren Production Centre, we are dedicated to delivering the very best customer experience.'[7]

Expectations were high when journalists finally got their hands on the long awaited MP4-12C: it promised breathtaking speed, superlative ride quality and handling in an everyday usable package. Despite ticking all of these boxes, the McLaren was almost universally criticised. According to *Autocar* magazine, it lacked the 'sense of occasion'[8] to match its pace; it 'failed to set pulses racing with its styling',[9] it was 'a touch clinical'[10] and lacked 'aural drama'. In summary, *Evo* magazine said it 'lacks emotional pull'.[11] In response to this criticism McLaren made a raft of changes before launch, designed to increase the 'emotional appeal'[12] of the car – a fruitier exhaust note among them.

To me, this illustrates the value of considering the emotional appeal of a product from the outset, especially when the purchase is fundamentally an emotional one: to spend £168,500 on a car is a decision that comes from the heart not the head. By the time the car is in production there is comparatively little that can be done: it can't be radically re-styled to create more visual drama. It also shows the clear value of testing the emotional response of customers before a product is launched to make sure that it hits the right notes.

We need to keep a clear picture in mind of how we want the customer to *feel* at a given stage of the experience, and use this as a reference point throughout the design process: we need to identify emotional success criteria to match the functional ones. Thinking this through will put you ahead of the competition. It is not always easy, but try to identify specific emotions if you can, for example we might want to incorporate an element of *positive surprise* when the customer un-boxes their product for the first time. In scenarios where a customer must absorb a lot of information it may be best that they are *relaxed* so that they can think clearly. For each stage of the customer journey, ask yourself *'How should the customer be feeling at this point?'*

To help frame the experience in this way, overleaf is a table of common positive or negative emotions that may apply to the experience.

Intensity

Emotions exist in part to attract our attention to a certain stimulus in our environment,[13] so the more intensely we feel an emotion, the less able we are to concentrate on other things.

A table of common emotions that may apply to your customer experience

NEGATIVE EMOTIONS	POSITIVE EMOTIONS
Anger	Acceptance
Annoyance	Admiration
Anxiety	Amazement
Apprehension	Anticipation
Boredom	Calmness
Disappointment	Delight
Disgust	Excitement
Distraction	Interest
Doubt	Joy
Embarrassment	Pride
Frustration	Relaxation
Neglect	Satisfaction
Regret	Surprise (positive)
Surprise (negative)	Trust

This dimension of emotion, known as arousal, is a critical factor to consider when designing a customer experience. It might be that the optimum experience at a particular stage is the absence of any noticeable emotion at all so that we can concentrate on a task like filling in a complex form, or setting up a product for the first time. When considering the emotional aspect of a stage of the customer journey, ask yourself '*Is the level of intensity appropriate for the tasks the customer must complete?*'

I have been a keen musician since childhood, and one thing my teachers have always emphasised is the importance of *dynamics* to a performance. Varying the volume and feel of the notes breathes life into the music. We can think about the customer experience in this way, looking to vary the nature and intensity of emotion at particular points to create 'wow moments' in the customer journey. Ask yourself '*How can we vary the emotions and their intensity to produce a more compelling experience?*'

Inception – an emotional cornucopia

I can think of few films in recent years that have generated the level of anticipation and discussion as Christopher Nolan's masterpiece *Inception*. The trailer performs its role perfectly, pulling the viewer in with stunning visuals and haunting music, but only hinting at the intricacies of the plot; it never gives the game away, generating interest through a series of intense but mysterious spectacles that seem almost totally divorced from one another. During the film itself the intricacies of the plot hold the audience in suspense, culminating in an ending left open to personal interpretation. Writing for the *New York Daily News*, critic Joe Neumaier said, '*Inception* is going to turn out to be like a cinematic Rubik's cube – audiences won't be able to put it down … The water cooler factor with '*Inception*' is that people want to suss it out with their co-workers who saw it, and that makes the uninitiated curious about what all the fuss is. And that will help drive box office sales.'[14] He wasn't wrong: *Inception* was box office gold, grossing over $825 million worldwide at the cinema.[15]

Eliminate negative emotions

The challenge for the emotional experience is not just to evoke the positive emotions, it is to avoid the negative ones. Anger, boredom or disappointment are but a few of the feelings that can ruin a customer experience. When I see brands appear on social media it is almost always a knee-jerk reaction to a negative emotion. When evaluating the emotional aspect of a stage of the customer's journey, ask yourself *'What would cause negative feelings? How can we prevent these from occurring?'*

It may also be the case that the customer arrives at an interaction in a heightened emotional state. Let's imagine they've lost their wallet and they need to contact their bank to cancel their credit card. At this point the customer is likely to be upset, angry, anxious and distracted. Success in this interaction requires not just allowing them to complete the task at hand – cancelling their cards – but also reducing the intensity of the feelings and pushing them towards more positive emotional states, such as *acceptance* and *trust*.

Since the stakes are high in this interaction, any emotional response is likely to be exaggerated: keeping the customer on hold, giving them bad news – 'your new card should be with you in 14 working days' – is likely to push them into a more intense emotion, from annoyance to anger, or from anger to rage. Yet this also affords a fantastic opportunity to generate greater positive emotions: trust might become admiration, surprise might become amazement. I for one would be pretty amazed if they answered the phone straight away and got a new card to me the next day at any location, even if I called in the evening. Framing an experience from an emotional perspective not only generates more empathy for the customer, it also helps identify new opportunities.

Philips Rationalizer Concept – an emotional mirror for traders

Teaming up with ABN-Amro, Philips have designed a concept piece called 'The Rationalizer', an emotion sensing system targeted at serious investors who trade online from home. The Rationalizer consists of two parts – a bracelet that measures the user's arousal level and the EmoBowl, a kind of ornament which acts as an 'emotion mirror', showing dynamic patterns of light, shifting from a pale yellow to a deep red, depending on the emotion. Why? According to Philips, 'Research shows that home investors do not act purely rationally: their behaviour is influenced by emotions, most notably fear and greed, which can compromise their ability to take an objective, factual stance. This insight led to the Rationalizer concept in which online traders are alerted when it may be wise to take a time-out, wind down and re-consider their actions.'[16]

Tracing emotions to principles

Most of the emotions that we experience during a customer journey can be directly traced back to the principles we have covered in this book: the better executed they are, the greater the emotional response. *Trust, surprise, disappointment, regret* and *acceptance*, for example, are all dependent on our expectations. *Frustration, anger, interest* and *satisfaction* are all a function of our objectives. The table below shows the most common emotions that occur during a customer experience and how they relate directly back to other topics we have already considered.

NEGATIVE EMOTIONS	PRINCIPLES AT WORK
Anger	Occurs when the pursuit of an *objective* is obstructed. May also be caused by inaccurate *expectations*, and a loss of *control*
Annoyance	Less intense than anger, annoyance occurs when the pursuit of an *objective* is hampered or when a task requires excessive *effort*
Anxiety	Strongly related to *stress*
Apprehension	This uncertainty relates back to *stress* factors, especially *competence*, and an over-abundance of choice
Boredom	Occurs when there is a lack of progress or stimulation. Can be traced back to *time on task*, which is a function of *effort*
Disappointment	The feeling of our *expectations* not being met
Distraction	Distraction is a component of *stress*
Doubt	This relates to uncertain *expectations* and also stress factors, especially *feedback*
Embarrassment	A violation of *social pleasure*. Also relates to *competence*
Frustration	Typically occurs when progress towards an *objective* is hampered, often as a result of *errors*
Neglect	Feeling neglected is a violation of *social pleasure*
Regret	A strong failure to meet *expectations*
Surprise (negative)	Occurs when *expectations* are not met

▶

POSITIVE EMOTIONS	PRINCIPLES AT WORK
Acceptance	Occurs when *expectations* are accurately set
Calmness	Felt in the absence of *stress*
Delight	Strongly related to *pleasure* and exceeding *expectations*
Excitement	A high arousal state, most often in anticipation – relates strongly to *expectation*
Interest	We are interested in those things that help us achieve our *objectives* and are sources of *pleasure*
Pride	Relates strongly to both *social pleasure* (status) and feeling in *control*
Relaxation	Felt in the absence of *stress*
Satisfaction	Occurs as a result of achieving our *objectives*
Surprise (positive)	Positive surprise occurs when *expectations* are exceeded
Trust	A function of consistently meeting *expectations*

When we see a brand or product that produces a strong positive emotional reaction, it is usually because the principles we have explored have combined to reinforce each other. To produce a compelling emotional reaction, the different principles must work together. Conversely, when there is a marked absence of emotional appeal, it may be because a specific principle has not been considered, or because the principles are undermining each other: mixed feelings do not compel action. This can be as simple as resisting that doughnut when we're trying to lose weight, or forgoing certain brands for ethical reasons even if we like the products. For a given stage of the customer journey, if you identify that a specific emotion must either be heavily promoted or avoided, you must make sure that everything in your toolkit is working together to make it happen.

Bang & Olufsen BeoSound 3000 – Surprise!

I remember the surprise I felt when I first encountered one of these CD players. The CD plays behind a pair of glass doors which slide apart as if by magic when you extend your hand towards the player. I've one of these players at home and it always fascinates my friends and their children. Their faces seem to light up when the doors magically open. The feeling of positive surprise is generated by the interplay of several principles. Any surprise is by definition unexpected, so obviously *expectations* play a part, but that is not enough for it to be positive feeling. The positive feeling comes from the *sensory* delight of watching the doors glide very precisely and from the feeling of *controlling* the technology with such a simple gesture. I also think it softens the personality of the device: to see something so sleek, cold and angular come to life in such a playful way adds to the surprise. One thing isn't a surprise though: this particular model is considered an industrial design icon and remained in production in various guises from 1994 to 2006 despite the amazing changes in technology we saw during that time.

Test emotional responses

We can do our best to design an interaction to provoke specific emotions, but to make sure we've nailed it we need to test the experience with customers to see if it elicits the appropriate emotional response. Fortunately, emotions can often be easily observed through our facial expressions and changes in tone of voice. During testing, look out for any observable emotional reaction and identify what stimulated the response. This kind of testing is invaluable, especially in eliminating negative responses from the customer that they may not articulate in verbal feedback.

Silverback – usability testing software

This great product has been invaluable to me in testing websites and software. It not only captures what users do on the screen – where they move the cursor and what they type – but also uses the webcam built into the laptop to capture the facial expressions of the user during a task. Often the video of the customer's face is more revealing than the actual interaction they have with the

▶

computer, showing their frustration, confusion, joy and interest. On one project, it was only when showing the CEO of the company a user's emotional reaction to his product that he acknowledged the problems with it!

Ferrari – 80 per cent of testing is to 'give the car a soul'

No discussion of emotional brands and products would be complete without a mention of Ferrari, possibly the most evocative brand of them all. Some see owning a Ferrari as the definitive symbol of success, to others it is the ultimate expression of Italian flair. For yet more the driving experience and racing heritage is what is at the root of the appeal. One thing is for sure, for many people Ferrari resolutely ticks all the boxes and reaps the benefits: the prancing horse inspires ferocious loyalty among car collectors and F1 fans alike. In May 2012 a 1962 Ferrari 250 GTO sold for £22.7 million.[17] Ferrari themselves are acutely aware that their success depends on emotional appeal. Comments from Ferrari test driver Raffaele De Simone are revealing: 'My job is to test the car and give a subjective evaluation ... this is a point that makes Ferrari special: don't trust only the numbers, because we sell emotion, not numbers ... just about 20 per cent of our testing is spent on performance ... we need to build cars that deliver emotion ... We work on feelings, on the senses – all five, the smell of the leather, the noise from the exhaust, the acceleration during gear shifting ... These are what I am 80 per cent focused on in the testing, to give soul to a car. That is not easy. It's much more difficult than going fast.'[18]

Do not be afraid of provoking a strong reaction

There are very few products that have a universal appeal. Even the most successful products have their detractors; in fact, often the more successful a brand is the less appeal it has for some. Their need to express their individuality means they can't abide anything with a mass appeal. There is a strong likelihood that as you increase the emotional appeal of your brand or product, you will also agitate the detractors. Don't worry about it. Remember that you are making stuff for the people who like your brand. Focus on satisfying them, and they will do the hard work of winning other people over through their passion. Be confident. You can't please everyone all of the time.

Crocs – love 'em or hate 'em

Few brands divide opinion like Crocs, the plastic shoe brand. People genuinely seem to love or hate them. Those who loathe them do so for two reasons: they say that Crocs look ugly and they don't identify with the people who wear them. If you are young and fashionable, sporting the same unflattering footwear as your mum wears while gardening is definitely not cool. Here the emotional response is caused by two reinforcing principles at work: the customer's identity is a mis-match for the product, and the visual design promotes negative feelings.

There are plenty of people who *really* love them though. They say they are comfortable to wear, they like the bright colours, and they rave about the practical benefits of the utilitarian design. For the Croc-lover the emotional reaction is promoted by sensory pleasure combined with the shoe satisfying their practical requirements – it satisfies their objectives. There is some bad news for Croc-haters the world over: in 2011 sales topped $1 billion, and over 100 million pairs of Crocs have been sold across 90 countries.[19]

Emotional attachment

Several years ago I took a three-month trip to Japan, Australia, New Zealand and the Cook Islands. I wanted a break from things, but also really wanted to develop my photography skills. I thought that being present amid some of the most beautiful scenery in the world with no agenda but taking photos would be an amazing, immersive experience, which it was.

I really wanted to develop my technique, so before the trip I sold my digital camera and lenses and bought an old Hasselblad V-series film camera, thinking it would force me to improve. The *craft* element of photography has always had a major appeal: I get a lot more satisfaction from getting the films back and seeing the images correctly exposed than I do from shooting loads of frames, looking at them on the screen on the back of the camera and then keeping the best one.

I found the camera an absolute joy to operate: the shutter has a unique and reassuring clunk to it, the bright viewfinder allows you to take in all of the scene, and when you pick one up you can feel its quality. Unlike modern cameras which all but take the picture for you, the Hasselblad puts the photographer in charge: all you get is shutter speed and aperture controls, and a button to take the picture. It doesn't even have a light meter to help you set the exposure. This made the whole process of taking an image much more engaging and rewarding.

During my trip, the camera worked faultlessly however much it got knocked around, and as anyone who uses one of these cameras will confirm, the quality of the pictures they take is stunning. Finally, and perhaps most importantly, over the course of the trip, the camera became a part of me. I became a huge fan of Hasselblad and everything they stood for. I am not alone: the V-series Hasselblad has a cult-like following, and has been in continuous production since 1948. Its popularity as a medium-format camera is almost unrivalled. Of the things I own, this camera is the one I have the most emotional attachment to. It was only during the course of my research that I realised my experience with the Hasselblad combined all the principles in this book in perfect harmony.

To feel an emotional attachment to a brand, product or service is the ultimate validation of a fantastic customer experience and the ultimate expression of the experience design principles that I believe in. To achieve this we must combine all the principles we have covered: the brand must reflect the customer's value and identity; the product must meet our expectations and fulfil our objectives; and every interaction with the business must be as pleasurable as possible.

Summary

- The way a product, brand or service makes us feel is critical to its success.

- Emotions can have specific 'action tendencies', so to encourage (or discourage) a specific behaviour we may need to evoke (or avoid) specific emotions.

- Having a target emotional state for each stage of the customer experience provides a goal to work towards that brings empathy and focus to the design process.

- Since emotions are often readily observable we can incorporate them into testing to validate our work, or identify opportunities for improvement.

- We not only need to promote positive emotions, but actively avoid negative ones too.

- When considering the emotional aspect of the experience we must consider how the intensity of feelings affects concentration.

- Most emotions we experience as customers can be traced back to the other principles in the book: *trust*, *surprise*, *disappointment*, *regret* and *acceptance* are all dependent on our expectations.

- To create strong emotional responses we must combine these principles effectively.

- Emotional attachment comes from successfully using all of the principles in this book.

14

Bringing it all together – the Apple customer experience

When I set out to write this book I did so with a slightly perverse determination that I would not use Apple as an example for anything. I felt it was lazy, or boring even; there are plenty of other businesses which offer fantastic customer experiences that we can learn from, yet don't receive anywhere near the same level of coverage.

As a designer Apple are as much a curse as a blessing, owing to their inescapable influence. Design and client meetings are dominated by them, even if the industry itself has nothing to do with consumer electronics. When Apple released their 'coverflow' system for swishing through music artwork on the iPod every client I worked with started demanding 'coverflow' interfaces on their websites. It didn't matter that it never worked especially well in the web context (Apple themselves didn't use it on their website for example), it's what they wanted. In a recent client discussion about providing a better in-store experience, the designer assigned to the project spent most of the briefing meeting talking about Apple's 'Genius bar' and how fantastic it was. There is less user-centered design than there is Apple-centered design these days. If I had my way I would ban their mention from any design discussion on projects in an effort to expand people's horizons.

And yet, in the context of this book, to ignore them on these grounds would be to do them a great disservice. Put simply there is no business that better embodies the principles that I advocate, and none which illustrates so well the success that can come from a relentless focus on the customer experience. At the time of writing Apple are the most valuable company in the world.[1]

It is no surprise that the world's most valuable company also have the world's most valuable brand.[2] Apple have developed a following that is often described as cult-like. At the launch of a new product many fans travel from far and wide, camping overnight to be the first to get their hands on the new release. Apple products are seen by consumers as fresh, modern, high-tech and cool. They are seen as the leaders rather than the followers. Few in consumer electronics can compete with this. As one commentator put it, 'We don't see anyone getting a Samsung tattoo.'[3]

Although their marketing is often as lauded as their products, their brand value has been achieved through consistently creating products and services that work better than those of their immediate competitors, rather than the cultivation of a particular image. I do not see one particular demographic for whom the iPod or iPhone have an appeal: these are universal products.

Whereas many businesses are keener than ever to include their customers in product development, Apple remain staunchly inner-directed, something I believe is key to their success. When asked in an interview how Apple know their consumers will want their products, design chief Sir Jonathan Ive replied, 'We don't do focus groups – that is the job of the designer. It's unfair to ask people who don't have a sense of the opportunities of tomorrow from the context of today to design.'[4] This is one area where competitors certainly could do better by following Apple's example. They are just as famous for saying no to things and ignoring customer requests as they are for advancing the state of the art, as was the case when they refused to support Adobe Flash on their mobile devices.[5] This is not the only area in which Apple have taken control away from the customer: the iPod was famously crippled to only allow content to flow into the device from one computer, and every app that is submitted to the app store is checked against rigorous guidelines before being offered for sale. Now that Apple is such a dominant player in content, no doubt we will see heated debate about their role as arbiter of what material we can or cannot view on their devices.

Apple's attention to detail is fastidious, my personal favourite being the small heartbeat light on the front of my laptop that makes it look like it's sleeping when the lid is closed. It's such a small touch but it really gives the laptop some personality. This attention extends along the whole customer journey from the retail experience, through un-boxing, using their products and onto any after-sales service.

Few other businesses have gone to the lengths that Apple have to make their products and services as effortless and stress free as possible to use, much of which has been possible by viewing the customer journey as a continuum rather than as individual features. When the iTunes store was launched it became all but effortless to buy music online, organise it into playlists and sync that content onto your iPod. Likewise, the well thought out back-up and restore function on the iPhone means that if you lose or upgrade your phone, you just plug it in and a few minutes later you have your new phone exactly as your old one was. Before Apple entered the market, most people moved their contacts from one device to another by copying them to the SIM card or re-typing them manually.

Comparing the range of Apple products to those of their competitors shows the value of having smaller product ranges: it becomes far easier to choose the product that best meets your needs. At the time of writing, there are two basic laptop models: the MacBook Air – small and light; and the MacBook Pro – the workhorse. There are two screen sizes available for each. Perhaps more impressive is that there is only one model of phone, yet at the time of writing their share of the US smart-phone market is 44.9 per cent.[6]

Apple tend to receive the most praise for the sensory experience of their products: from the original colourful iMac through to the studied minimalism of its latest incarnation, Apple have designed products that delight the senses. Unlike the ugly, beige boxes of their competitors, a Mac could take pride of place in the living room. With the introduction of the iPhone, iPod Touch and iPad, Apple moved gestural touch-based interfaces from sci-fi into mainstream reality, but where they perhaps deserve more praise is for how they have made these devices accessible to those with sensory impairments. Their phone is completely usable by blind people, using a feature called 'VoiceOver', which reads out the labels of any navigation items that the user touches. They have even extended this functionality to the camera application: if you switch

VoiceOver on, then launch the camera and point it at a person it will tell you when they are in the frame. I tried this and it said, 'One face. Large face. Centre. Autofocused.' I then double tapped to take the picture.

A few years ago, a friend of mine, Andy, sent me a message about an incident he'd had with some software on his Mac. After failing to rectify the fault, he decided to take a punt and e-mailed Steve Jobs with his problem. The following day he received a reply from the director of the product division asking for his location so he could fly one of the developers of the software out from California to his home (in Liverpool) to help rectify the problem. This is an extreme example, and yet when I asked friends for examples of outstanding customer service, Apple are mentioned more than any other brand. In a world where most seem to want to quibble over every penny, it seems that Apple employees want their customers to leave the Genius Bar with their product working as it should, feeling well looked after.

Speaking to the BBC after receiving his knighthood, Sir Jonathan Ive's comments about their goals as a company were revealing: 'It's to try to design the very best products that we possibly can ... We're very disciplined, very focused, and very clear, across the company – that is our goal ... If we manage to do that then there are a number of consequences. People will like the product, hopefully they'll buy the product, and then we will make some money ... The goal isn't to make money, the goal is to try to develop the very best products that we can.'[7] This is something we can all aspire to do.

15

Final thoughts

From the outset, this book was written in the spirit of giving something back to a profession that has give me so much over the years; however, I also believe that the principles that I have explored have much to contribute beyond the immediate arena of customer experience. How might they be used to create more rewarding and pleasant working environments, for example? I also see strong parallels between the business–customer relationship and that of governments and their citizens. How might these principles be used by governments to improve the quality of life of their citizens in meaningful ways? Will we one day experience a taxation system that mere mortals can comprehend? On a basic level, we are all united in our consumption of the planet's resources. How might we put these principles to work to minimise the waste of materials or food? These issues are as much the designer's responsibility as the consumer's, if not more so, and I believe these principles have much to contribute in this area too.

Finally, I wish to thank you for purchasing and reading this book. If you have any comments, questions or feedback, good or bad on any aspect of this book, I would love to hear from you. Please do not hesitate to e-mail me at mw@mattwatkinson.co.uk.

Notes

Preface

1   Musashi, M., translated by Cleary, T. (1993) *The Book of Five Rings*, Boston: Shambhala Productions.

Chapter 1

1   http://www.independent.co.uk/extras/indybest/food-drink/the-50-best-breakfast-spots-6256963.html
2   http://www.waitrose.com/content/waitrose/en/home/inspiration/waitrose_kitchen_feb/archive/river_cafe_romance.html
3   http://www.guardian.co.uk/music/2012/feb/13/whitney-houston-album-price
4   http://www.digitalspy.co.uk/music/news/a365322/whitney-houston-death-apple-criticised-after-albums-price-boost.html
5   http://stakeholders.ofcom.org.uk/consultations/unexpectedly-high-bills/statement/
6   http://media.ofcom.org.uk/2012/03/01/tacking-unexpectedly-high-phone-bills/
7   http://www.telegraph.co.uk/finance/personalfinance/consumertips/banking/9019839/Bank-overdraft-fees-leave-even-maths-PhD-baffled.html
8   http://www.bbc.co.uk/news/business-16002022
9   Sparke, P. (2009) *The Genius of Design*, London: Quadrille Publishing
10 Friedman, M. (1970) 'The social responsibility of business is to increase its profits', *The New York Times Magazine*, 13 September
11 Jensen, M.C. and Meckling, W.H. (1976) 'Theory of the Firm: Managerial Behaviour, Agency Costs and Ownership Structure', *Journal of Financial Economics* 3, no. 4: 305–360
12 Martin, R.L. (2011) *Fixing the Game*, Boston: Harvard Business School Publishing, p. 99
13 Ibid. p. 36
14 Ibid. p. 85
15 http://thecustomerblog.co.uk/2011/09/12/bad-customer-experience-power-to-the-people/
16 http://www.christophevanbael.com/dutch-comedian-starts-campaign-against-helpdesk-terror/
17 http://www.t-mobile.nl/persoonlijk/htdocs/popup/youpvanthek.aspx
18 http://www.telecompaper.com/news/belgian-operators-sign-customer-service-charter
19 Jones, D. (2012) *Who Cares Wins*, London: Pearson Education, p. 26
20 Ibid. p. 28
21 http://www.100daysofdesign.com/?p=277
22 Esslinger, H. (2009) *A Fine Line*, San Francisco: Jossey Bass, p. 84
23 Ibid. pp. 2–4
24 Drucker, P.F. (1955) *The Practice of Management*, London: Heinemann
25 http://www.bbc.co.uk/news/business-16812545

Chapter 2

1   Norman, D.A. (2004) *Emotional Design*, New York: Basic Books
2   http://www.kenrockwell.com/tech/7.htm
3   Patnaik, D. and Mortensen, P. (2009) *Wired to Care*, New Jersey: FT Press, p. 23

4   Funnel, W. (1998) 'Accounting in the service of the Holocaust', *Critical Perspectives on Accounting* 8, 435–464
5   DeMarco, T. (2001) *Slack*, New York: Dorset House, p. xii
6   Fried, J. and Heinemeier Hansson, D. (2010) *Rework*, p. 144
7   Rowan, D. (2012) 'Here for the long haul: Corporate long-termism', *Wired Magazine*, UK edition January 2012, p. 121
8   Ibid. p. 37
9   DeMarco, T., Hruschka, P. *et al.* (2008) *Adrenaline Junkies and Template Zombies*, New York: Dorset House, p. 138
10 Isaacson, W. (2011) *Steve Jobs*, London: Little, Brown, p. 342
11 Reichheld, F. and Markey, R. (2011) *The Ultimate Question 2.0*, Boston: Harvard Business School Publishing, pp. 21–40
12 Martin, R.L. (2011) *Fixing the Game*, Boston: Harvard Business School Publishing, p. 31
13 Ibid. pp. 4–6
14 Ibid. p. 62

Chapter 3
1   Michalko, M. (2006) *Thinkertoys*, Berkley: Ten Speed Press, p. xvii
2   Liker, J.K. (2004) *The Toyota Way*, New York: McGraw-Hill, p. 253

Chapter 4
1   Baudrillard, J. (1981) *For a Critique of the Political Economy of the Sign*, New York: Telos Press Ltd, pp. 63–66
2   http://www.scotsman.com/news/uk/poor-parenting-and-designer-brand-greed-caused-london-riots-claims-report-1-2199666?commentssort=0
3   Whyte, W.H. (1956) *The Organisation Man*, New York: Simon and Schuster
4   Reisman, D. (1961) *The Lonely Crowd*, New Haven CT: Yale University Press, p. 11
5   Ibid. p. 11
6   Ibid. p. 16
7   Ibid. p. 22
8   Ibid. p. 25
9   Ibid. p. 32
10 Ibid. p.190
11 Ibid. p. 209
12 http://phx.corporate-ir.net/phoenix.zhtml?c=61701&p=irol-newsArticle_print&ID=1301464&highlight=
13 http://www.iwc.com/forum/en/
14 http://www.etsy.com/about?ref=ft_about
15 Ibid.
16 Ibid.
17 http://www.youtube.com/watch?v=3iaTEgoezNQ
18 Walker, R. (2008) *Buying In – What We Buy And Who We Are*, New York: Random House, p. 46
19 Chouinard, Y. (2006) *Let My People Go Surfing*, New York: Penguin Books, pp. 85–116
20 http://www.johnlewis.com/Magazine/Feature.aspx?Id=517

Chapter 5
1   http://en.wikipedia.org/wiki/What_Women_Want
2   Fried, J. and Heinemeier Hansson, D. (2010) *Rework*, p.34
3   Patnaik, D. and Mortensen, P. (2009) *Wired to Care*, New Jersey: FT Press, p.67

4 Cope, N. (2003) *The Seven Cs of Consulting*, Harlow: FT Prentice Hall, pp. 103–114
5 Mulder, S. and Yaar, Z. (2007) *The User is Always Right*, Berkeley: New Riders, p. 38
6 Cooper, A., Reimann, R. and Cronin, D. (2007) *About Face 3*, Indianapolis: Wiley Publishing, pp. 15–17
7 Ibid. p.16
8 Merlin, B. (2007) *The Complete Stanislavsky Toolkit*, London: Nick Hern Books, p. 60
9 Ibid. pp. 219–226
10 http://www.bbc.co.uk/news/business-16625725
11 http://www.bbc.co.uk/news/technology-17658264
12 http://online.wsj.com/article/SB10001424052970204831304576594524134179668.html
13 http://www.telegraph.co.uk/technology/facebook/8240095/Will-Facebook-conquer-the-world.html
14 http://www.businessweek.com/news/2011-12-16/amazon-says-kindle-sales-topping-1-million-devices-a-week.html
15 Ibid. pp. 91–97
16 Ibid. pp. 73–90
17 Ibid. p. 157
18 Ibid. p. 156

Chapter 6

1 Greene, R. (2003) *The Concise Art of Seduction*, London: Profile Books, p. 115
2 http://www.teamsky.com/article/0,27290,17547_5792058,00.html
3 http://www.guardian.co.uk/politics/reality-check-with-polly-curtis/2012/apr/18/tesco-retail?intcmp=239
4 Ibid.
5 http://www.thesundaytimes.co.uk/sto/comment/columns/article1021523.ece (accessible by subscription only)
6 http://www.guardian.co.uk/business/2012/apr/18/tesco-uk-profits-fall-makeover

Chapter 7

1 http://www.accenture.com/SiteCollectionDocuments/PDF/EEtimesreprint16803e.pdf
2 http://www.theinquirer.net/inquirer/news/1032100/per-cent-returned-electronics
3 Kahneman, D. (2011) *Thinking Fast and Slow*, London: Allen Lane, p. 381
4 Ibid. p. 381
5 Reason, J. (1990) *Human Error,* New York: Cambridge University Press, p. 68
6 http://www.thestar.com/article/232343
7 Ibid. pp. 380–382
8 http://news.bbc.co.uk/1/hi/business/7532660.stm
9 http://news.bbc.co.uk/1/hi/technology/7964459.stm

Chapter 8

1 Rams, D. (1995) *Less But Better*, Hamburg: Jo Klatt Design + Design Verlag, p. 7
2 Ibid
3 Maeda, J. (2006) *The Laws of Simplicity*, Cambridge, Massachusetts: MIT Press, p. 1
4 Strunk Jr, W. and White, E.B. (1999) *The Elements of Style*, fourth edn, New York: Longman
5 Jenson, S. (2002) *The Simplicity Shift*, Cambridge: Cambridge University Press, pp. 81–82
6 Ibid, p. 82
7 Neuhart, J., Neuhart, M., *et al.* (1989) *Eames Design*, New York: Harry N. Abrams, Inc., p. 15

8   Jenson, S. (2002) *The Simplicity Shift*, Cambridge: Cambridge University Press, pp. 14–16.
9   http://www.nokia.com/gb-en/products/all-products/ (accessed 27 June 2012)
10   Lidwell, W., Holden, K. and Butler, J. (2003) *Universal Principles of Design*, Gloucester, Massachusetts: Rockport Publishers, p. 154
11   Maeda, J. (2006) *The Laws of Simplicity*, Cambridge, Massachusetts: MIT Press, p. 84
12   http://www.amazon.co.uk/kindle

Chapter 9

1   Reason, J. (2008) *The Human Contribution – Unsafe Acts, Accidents and Heroic Recoveries*, Farnham: Ashgate Publishing, pp. 29–46
2   Ibid. pp. 34–38
3   Wickens, C.D. and Hollands, J.G. (2000) *Human Psychology and Engineering Performance*, New Jersey: Prentice Hall, pp. 490–491
4   Schwartz, B. (2004) *The Paradox of Choice*, New York: Harper Perennial, pp. 2–75
5   Carnegie, D. (1984) *How to Stop Worrying and Start Living*, London: Vermilion, p. 53

Chapter 10

1   Lidwell, W., Holden, K. and Butler, J. (2003) *Universal Principles of Design*, Gloucester, Massachusetts: Rockport Publishers, p. 18
2   Peck, J. 'Does Touch Matter? Insights From Haptic Research In Marketing', within Krishna, A. (2010) *Sensory Marketing*, New York: Routledge, p. 24
3   Lwin, M.O. and Wijaya, M. 'Do Scents Evoke the Same Feelings Across Cultures?' 'Exploring the Role of Emotions', within Krishna, A. (2010) *Sensory Marketing*, New York: Routledge, p. 113
4   Herz, R.S. 'The Emotional, Cognitive, and Biological Basics of Olfaction', within Krishna, A. (2010) *Sensory Marketing*, New York: Routledge p. 101
5   http://adage.com/article/viewpoint/follow-nose-marketing-evolution/103233/
6   http://www.independent.co.uk/arts-entertainment/music/features/mind-the-bach-classical-music-on-the-underground-800483.html
7   http://www.businessweek.com/magazine/content/04_47/b3909094_mz017.htm
8   Cracknell, A. (2011) *The Real Mad Men*, London: Quercus, p. 45
9   http://www.thefatduck.co.uk/Heston-Blumenthal/Our-Philosophy/
10   http://www.thefatduck.co.uk/Heston-Blumenthal/Our-Awards/
11   http://www.toniandguy.com/pages/category/about-us/our-story
12   http://www.oxo.com/OurAwards.aspx
13   http://www.oxo.com/aboutOXO.aspx
14   http://www.wired.com/wired/archive/12.12/traffic.html
15   http://www.vivobarefoot.com/uk/about-us/

Chapter 11

1   http://www.closedpubs.co.uk/
2   Reisman, D. (1961) *The Lonely Crowd*, New Haven CT: Yale University Press, p. 188
3   http://www.guardian.co.uk/books/2011/feb/02/waterstones-to-close-20-branches
4   http://www.ft.com/cms/s/0/4d1551a8-2627-11e1-9ed3-00144feabdc0.html
5   http://www.trailfinders.com/media.nsf/awards?readform
6   http://www.forbes.com/2009/10/30/simon-cooper-ritz-leadership-ceonetwork-hotels.html
7   De Botton, A. (2005) *Status* Anxiety, London: Penguin Books
8   http://uxmag.com/articles/the-impossible-bloomberg-makeover
9   Tiger, L. (2000) *The Pursuit of Pleasure*, New Jersey: Transaction Publishers, p. 258

10 http://www.independent.co.uk/life-style/health-and-families/health-news/the-musthave-buggy-that-costs-more-than-a-secondhand-car-2266945.html

Chapter 12
1 Deci, I.L. and Ryan, R.M. (1985) *Intrinsic motivation and self-determination in human behaviour*, New York: Plenum Press
2 http://www.dailymobile.net/2009/09/20/power-to-you-vodafones-new-brand-add-campaign/
3 http://basecamp.com/pricing
4 http://basecamp.com/
5 Chouinard, Y. (2006) *Let My People Go Surfing*, New York: Penguin Books, p. 90
6 http://www.sony.co.uk/hub/vaio-laptops (accessed 28 June 2012)
7 Ibid.
8 http://www.sony.co.uk/product/vn-c-series/vpccb3p1e
9 http://www.buildabear.co.uk/aboutus/ourcompany/ourstory.aspx
10 http://money.cnn.com/magazines/fortune/best-companies/2012/snapshots/62.html

Chapter 13
1 http://www.bbc.co.uk/news/business-15550428
2 http://www.bbc.co.uk/news/business-18015791
3 http://www.telegraph.co.uk/finance/jobs/9193958/Sony-to-cut-10000-jobs-worldwide.html
4 Niedenthal, P.M., Krauth-Gruber, S. and Ric, F. (2006) *Psychology of Emotion*, New York: Psychology Press, pp. 63–76
5 Ibid. p. 66
6 Ibid. p. 66
7 http://www.mclaren.com/home/what-we-do
8 http://www.autocar.co.uk/car-news/new-cars/mclaren-tweak-mp4-12c
9 http://www.autocar.co.uk/car-review/mclaren/mp4-12c/design
10 http://www.autocar.co.uk/car-review/mclaren/mp4-12c
11 http://www.evo.co.uk/news/evonews/269944/ferrari_458_beats_mclaren_mp412c.html
12 See note 8 above
13 Evans, D. (2001) *Emotion – A Very Short Introduction*, Oxford: Oxford University Press, p. 77
14 http://www.popeater.com/2010/07/23/inception-box-office/
15 http://boxofficemojo.com/movies/?page=main&id=inception.htm
16 http://www.newscenter.philips.com/main/standard/news/articles/20091013_rationalizer.wpd
17 http://www.dailymail.co.uk/news/article-2153738/Ferrari-built-Stirling-Moss-sells-record-breaking-22-7million-classic-car-auction.html
18 http://www.thenational.ae/lifestyle/motoring/test-driver-helps-puts-the-emotion-in-ferraris#page2
19 http://company.crocs.com/news/news-releases/

Chapter 14
1 http://www.telegraph.co.uk/technology/apple/9037186/Apple-is-worlds-most-valuable-company-after-iPhone-frenzy-drives-record-profits.html
2 http://www.forbes.com/sites/timworstall/2012/05/22/apple-still-the-worlds-most-valuable-brand/
3 http://www.informationweek.com/news/mobility/smart_phones/232301387

4   http://www.standard.co.uk/lifestyle/london-life/sir-jonathan-ive-the-iman-cometh-7562170.html
5   http://www.apple.com/hotnews/thoughts-on-flash/
6   http://www.telegraph.co.uk/technology/apple/9038087/Apple-iPhone-market-share-outpacing-Android.html
7   http://www.bbc.co.uk/news/technology-18188670

Index